A Hispanic Heritage
Series III

*A guide to juvenile books
about Hispanic people and cultures*

Isabel Schon

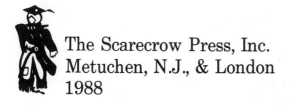

The Scarecrow Press, Inc.
Metuchen, N.J., & London
1988

OTHER SCARECROW TITLES BY ISABEL SCHON

Basic Collection of Children's Books in Spanish
A Bicultural Heritage
Books in Spanish for Children and Young Adults
Books in Spanish for Children and Young Adults, Series II
Books in Spanish for Children and Young Adults, Series III
Books in Spanish for Children and Young Adults, Series IV
A Hispanic Heritage
A Hispanic Heritage, Series II

Library of Congress Cataloging-in-Publication Data

Schon, Isabel.
    A Hispanic heritage, series III : a guide to juvenile books
about Hispanic people and cultures / Isabel Schon.
        p.   cm.
    Includes indexes.
    ISBN 0-8108-2133-8
    1. Latin America--Juvenile literature--Bibliography. 2.
Spain--Juvenile literature--Bibliography. 3. Hispanic Ameri-
cans--Juvenile literature--Bibliography. I. Title. II. Title:
Hispanic heritage, series 3. III. Title: Hispanic heritage,
series three.
Z1609.C5S363   1988
[F1408]
016.98--dc19   88-18094

To my parents,
Dr. Oswald Schon
and
Mrs. Anita Schon

to my husband,
Dr. Richard R. Chalquest

to my daughter,
Verita

TABLE OF CONTENTS

PREFACE

Like its predecessors, this book is designed as an aid for librarians and teachers who are interested in exposing students to the cultures of Hispanic people through books for children and adolescents.

These books are intended to provide students in kindergarten through high school with an understanding of, and an appreciation for, the people, history, art, and political, social, and economic problems of Argentina, Bolivia, Chile, Colombia, Costa Rica, Cuba, Ecuador, El Salvador, Guatemala, Honduras, Mexico, Nicaragua, Panama, Peru, Puerto Rico, Spain, Venezuela, and the Hispanic heritage people in the United States.

A Hispanic Heritage, Series III is arranged into chapters that explore specific countries and cultures, as well as one each on Central and Latin America as a whole. The books are listed in alphabetical order by author surname. These countries are representative of Hispanic cultures and should assist librarians, teachers, and students in their efforts to better know and comprehend the marvelous richness and diversity of the cultures of Hispanic people.

Although I have attempted to include most in-print books in English published since 1984 in the United States that relate to the countries and people listed above, as well as general books on Latin America, I undoubtedly have missed some important books. Their omission is due to unavailability, nonexistence at the time of compilation, or my own lack of awareness of them. However, not all the books listed are recommended titles. For the convenience of the reader, I have marked with an asterisk (*) noteworthy books. These books contain recent information, as well as being entertaining and possessing high potential for interesting or involving the reader. I urge readers to be especially critical of many books that contain obsolete information or that expose a very limited or one-sided view of Hispanic people, customs, or countries. Students should be encouraged to read books that provide objective information and that present new insights into Hispanic people and cultures.

As any librarian or teacher knows, it is very difficult to assign a grade level to a book. And even though I have done so for the convenience of some teachers or students, please use the grade level only as a tentative guideline. An arbitrary grade level should never stop a student from reading or viewing a book that he or she expresses interest in.

In the annotations I have expressed my personal opinions of the books, emphasizing what I believe are the strengths or weaknesses of each. I have summarized, criticized, and/ or highlighted specific ideas explored in the books about Hispanic countries and people.

In anticipation of user needs I have provided three indexes: an author index; a subject index, including references and cross-references; and a title index.

It is my hope that this book will encourage readers, librarians, teachers, and even publishers to expand their interests into the fascinating cultures of Hispanic people both in the United States and abroad.

I wish to express my appreciation to the Department of Reading Education and Library Science, Arizona State University, for its support; to the professional staffs of the University Library, Arizona State University, and San Diego Public Library--La Jolla Branch, for their continued assistance; and to Mrs. Carolyn Painter and Ms. Barbara Quarles for their marvelous cooperation.

Isabel Schon, Ph.D.
Professor in Library Science
Arizona State University, Tempe
December 1987

A HISPANIC HERITAGE
Series III

A Guide to Juvenile Books
About Hispanic People and Cultures

ARGENTINA

Borges, Jorge Luis, and Roberto Alifano. Twenty-four Conversations with Borges, Including a Selection of Poems: Interviews by Roberto Alifano, 1981-1983. Housatonic, MA: Lascaux Publishers, 1984. 157 p. Distributed by Grove Press. ISBN: 0-394-62192-1. $8.95. Gr. 10-adult.

These are twenty-four brief conversations with Borges recorded between 1981 and 1983. In them, Borges candidly talks about the problems of modern-day Argentina, such as corruption, the moral crisis, lack of democracy and others; his visit to Japan, which he calls "the most civilized country that I've known" (p. 17); and his thoughts and impressions of numerous Hispanic and English-language authors. In addition, it includes thirty-four newly translated poems by Borges.

Cortínez, Carlos, ed. Borges the Poet. Fayetteville: The University of Arkansas Press, 1986. 353 p. ISBN: 0-938626-37-X. $23.00. Gr. 9-adult.

Three discussions with Borges on Emily Dickinson, Hispanic Literature and English and North American Literature, as well as twenty-four essays on Borges's poetry written by well-known literary critics and friends of Borges, such as Willis Barnstone and María Kodama, provide a fascinating portrait of Borges the man and the poet. Admirers of Borges will be delighted with the poet's sincere humility and will be interested to learn about his favorite authors: "Jorge Guillén seems to me the greatest poet in the Spanish language" (p. 37) and "to me the supreme prose writer in the Spanish language is Alfonso Reyes" (p. 41). This is definitely a touching literary view of Borges, the poet.

Hintz, Martin. <u>Argentina</u>. (Enchantment of the World) Chicago: Children's Press, 1985, 128 p. ISBN: 0-516-02752-2.
$14.95. Gr. 4-8.

Outstanding photographs in color make this introductory
book to Argentina's geography, history, economy, people
and the arts a pleasant visual experience. Even though
the narrative provides important basic information about
Argentina, it sometimes oversimplifies or uses vague ter-
minology such as "confusing, perhaps, if you take only
a quick look" (p. 13), without further explanations. An
appendix contains most useful "Mini-facts at a Glance" as
well as "Important Dates and People" section.

*Huber, Alex. <u>We Live in Argentina</u>. (Living Here Series)
New York: The Bookwright Press, 1984. 60 p. ISBN:
0-531-03793-2. $9.90. Gr. 4-8.

Like other titles in this series, this book includes twenty-
six first-person interviews of people from Argentina who
describe their lives, occupations and the area of the country in which they live. Outstanding, colorful photographs
complement the informative two-page interviews. In contrast to other titles in this series, the people interviewed
from Argentina represent a true cross-section of people:
truck driver, museum guide, doctor, TV broadcaster, gaucho,
lawyer, farmer, and others, making this book a well-
balanced introduction to Argentina and its people.

Lye, Keith. <u>Take a Trip to Argentina</u>. (Take a Trip) New
York: Franklin Watts, 1986. 32 p. ISBN: 0-531-101940
$9.40. Gr. 2-4.

As a simple introduction to the geography of Argentina,
this easy-to-read book should appeal to young readers in
search of an attractive overview of some of the sites, land-
scapes and cities of Argentina. Spectacular, full-color
photographs and maps covey the beauty and diversity of
Argentina. The only weakness in this otherwise outstanding introductory book is that it is written more like a travel
guide to Argentina than as an introduction to the Argentine
people and how they live.

Moon, Bernice and Cliff. Argentina Is My Country. (My
  Country) New York: Marshall Cavendish, 1986. 60 p.
  ISBN: 0-86307-470-7. $10.00. Gr. 3-6.

Through twenty-six first person accounts, young readers
will learn about life in the cities, factories and farms of
Argentina. Carefully selected photographs in color and a
simple text describe the life of a student, farmer, café
owner, gaucho, winemaker, tango dancer, doctor, chocolate
factory worker and many others. Like other titles in this
series, this is a pleasant way to expose young readers
to life in Argentina.

Partnoy, Alicia. The Little School: Tales of Disappearance
  & Survival in Argentina. Pittsburgh, PA: Cleis Press,
  1986. 136 p. ISBN: 9-939416-08-5. $15.95. Gr. 10-adult.

Readers will be moved by this collection of "tales" that
recount the author's experiences during her imprisonment
in "the little school" where many young Argentines were
kidnapped, jailed, tortured and sometimes murdered because of their political beliefs. The author states in the
introduction that almost "30,000 Argentines 'disappeared'
between 1976 and 1979, the most oppressive years of the
military rule" (p. 11). This is indeed a pathetic testimony
to the abuses committed by military governments in South
America.

Strange, Ian J. The Falklands: South Atlantic Islands. Map
  and Photographs by the author. New York: Dodd, Mead
  & Co., 1985. 160 p. ISBN: 0-396-08616-0. $15.95.
  Gr. 6-9.

Through the author's long-term fascination with the wildlife of the Falkland Islands, the reader is exposed to the
islands' natural environment--their birds and animals--and
to the need for preserving the ecological balance for the
wildlife. Excellent black-and-white and color photographs
further attest to the natural beauty of the Falklands. In
addition, the author provides historical background, as
well as information on sheep ranching, fisheries, early
whaling activity and farming. The last chapter discusses
the conflict with Argentina in 1982 from the perspective

of a loyal British subject. As an introduction to the wildlife of the Falkland Islands, this book will excite most
readers. The other chapters, however, are unclear and
prosaic.

Unger, Douglas. El Yanqui. New York: Harper & Row
Publishers, 1986. 300 p. ISBN: 0-06-015645-9. $16.95.
Gr. 9-adult.

A longhaired American teenager who uses drugs and
dresses like a hippie is suddenly adopted by a wealthy
Argentine family through a student exchange program.
Thus begins this coming-of-age novel set in Argentina in
the 1960s. Readers will enjoy this teenager's experiences
with a new family, in another country, where he must
learn to deal with different customs and values. Unfortunately, there are too many coincidences in this powerful
novel that ignore the reality of life among the upper
classes of Argentina. The young man's sexual encounters
and personal doubts are indeed real. The misuse of the
Spanish language, however, further detracts from the
novel's impact.

Bolivia in Pictures. (Visual Geography Series) Minneapolis:
  Lerner Publications Company, 1987. 64 p. ISBN: 0-8225-
  1808-2. $9.95. Gr. 5-10.

Bolivia's land, history, government, people and economy
are described through numerous black-and-white and color
photographs and a direct, easy-to-read text. This updated
edition emphasizes many of the serious problems of Bolivia
today, such as its poverty and the growing and trading of
dangerous narcotic drugs as well as other facts: "The air
is so thin that La Paz does not even have a fire department
because there is not enough oxygen in the air to spread
flames" (p. 18).

Cross, Gillian. Born of the Sun. New York: Holiday House,
  Inc., 1983. 229 p. ISBN: 0-8234-0528-1. $11.95. Gr.
  8-10.

Paula, who is attending a boarding school in England, is
suddenly taken out of school and hastily planning an expedition with her famous father and explorer, Karel Staszic,
her mother, and a young, flippant photographer to the lost
city of Atahualpa in Peru. There is much adventure and
excitement in this story that takes place in high mountains,
dark jungles, and dangerous forests. Especially, as Paula
notices her father's irrational behavior that results in a
guide's death and other misfortunes for the unusual group
of explorers. Some readers may enjoy the excitement with
the added love story between an adventurous explorer
and a strong, capable woman. Yet, admirers of the Incas
will not be thrilled to read of the Incas as "a tribe of
mysterious healers" who guard the lost city of the Incas,
"a city that was prepared for Atahualpa, before the

Spanish murdered him" (p. 82). The exotic setting definitely creates exciting action and self-examining characters,
but it is a disappointment to those of us who admire the
Incas as more than occult healers.

St. John, Jetty. A Family in Bolivia. Photos by José Armando
Araneda. Minneapolis: Lerner Publications Company, 1986.
31 p. ISBN: 0-8225-1670-5. $8.95. Gr. 3-6.

The home, customs, work, school and amusements of a
Bolivian boy and his family who live on an island in a high
lake in the Andes are described through excellent photographs in color and an easy-to-read text. This is a
pleasing introduction to the life of the Indians from Bolivia.

CENTRAL AMERICA

See also Latin America, Costa Rica, El Salvador, Guatemala, Honduras, Nicaragua, and Panama.

Alexander, Lloyd. The El Dorado Adventure. New York:
E. P. Dutton, 1987. 164 p. ISBN: 0-525-44313-4.
$12.95. Gr. 6-10.

Vesper Holly, a brave and intelligent young woman, and
her loyal guardian, Professor Brinton Garrett, embark
on a dangerous journey to Central America, where she
has inherited valuable property. Upon arrival in the
tiny republic of El Dorado, she learns that a most un-
scrupulous Frenchman, Alain de Rochefort, is deter-
mined to purchase her estate. Amid an exotic background of the tropic in the 1870s and with the assistance
of the Chirica Indians, the young heroine succeeds in
stopping the villain and saving the Chiricas' homeland.
There is much adventure, excitement and intelligent women
successes in this tale, but as a novel about Central America it leaves much to be desired.

Berryman, Phillip. Inside Central America. New York:
Pantheon Books, 1985. 166 p. ISBN: 0-394-72943-9.
$5.95. Gr. 9-adult.

The author, the Central American representative for the
American Friends Service Committee, states that his pur-
poses are to present an outline of the main issues inside
Central America and "to provide both factual information
and a basis for interpretation," and, he "indicates
how steadily U.S. involvement, far from addressing

Central America's real problems, has prolonged and intensified the conflicts, and has led to a U.S.-sponsored war in Central America" (p. 33). This is one more of the many narratives that insist that "United States policies have helped aggravate the conflicts and their causes" (p. 128).

Blackman, Morris, and others, eds. Confronting Revolution: Security Through Diplomacy in Central America. New York: Pantheon Books, 1986. 438 p. ISBN: 0-394-55351-9. $22.95. Gr. 10-adult.

As stated in the preface, the fifteen authors and editors of this book came together in the Fall of 1982 "out of a deep concern to contribute to intelligent debate about United States foreign policy toward Central America" (p. vii). In fourteen chapters, they examine individual Central American countries as well as the roles of Cuba, the Soviet Union, Mexico, Venezuela and the United States. As is to be expected, the authors discuss the many failures of American policy and conclude that "the United States needs a policy for Central America that is designed to meet the limited security problems posed by the regional conflict, and does so as much as possible by diplomacy rather than the reflexive use of force; that shows a strict preference for democracy rather than for one variety of authoritarianism over another, but does not seek to impose that preference by force; and that works to encourage structural economic and social change that addresses the real roots of the region's political unrest" (p. 368). One would certainly like to believe that the problems of Central America are that easily resolved.

Central America: Opposing Viewpoints. Edited by David L. Bender and others. (Opposing Viewpoints Series) St. Paul, MN: Greehaven Press, 1984. 244 p. ISBN: 0-89908-322-6. $5.95. Gr. 10-adult.

The purpose of this book is to present balanced, opposing points of view on complex and sensitive issues regarding Central America. Articles from magazines, journals, books and newspapers as well as statements and position papers from a wide range of individuals, organizations and governments discuss questions that relate to U.S. national

security, the practicability and morality of U.S. involvement in Central America, and the possibilities for peace
in the region. Although many of the articles sound like
political propaganda, either from the Right or Left, and
use many words to say nothing, a few offer insightful
truths/perspectives about the many problematic issues
facing the United States in Central America today. Each
of the five chapters ends with "a basic reading and think-
ing skill" section that assists readers in critically evaluating such issues as ethnocentrism and distinguishing primary from secondary sources. The most valuable aspect
of this book is that it pulls articles from many sources
and differing points of view into one volume.

Chace, James. Endless War: How We Got Involved in Central
   America--and What Can Be Done. New York: Vintage
   Books, 1984. 144 p. ISBN: 0-394-72779-7. $3.94.
   Gr. 10-adult.

This is a strong indictment of U.S. policy toward Central
America beginning with Thomas Jefferson up to the Reagan
administration. Apparently, "a lengthy trip to Central
America" in the Spring of 1982 gave the author the insights
to what he believes are the anxieties and fears that have
dominated U.S. policy in Central America and to propose
solutions in some cases--demilitarization--and impossible
solutions in other cases such as in El Salvador. It is
obvious that Mr. Chace believes that it is the United States'
responsibility to improve the economies of Central America
and Mexico, encourage the growth of democracy and create
stability in those countries. Thus, according to him, it is
easy to question America's "credibility" because of "the
obtuseness of her foreign policy" (p. 136). Why does he
not mention the internal problems of those countries that
continue to foster incredible abuses of power, gross mismanagement, callous corruption and dismal poverty? Perhaps because it is simpler to blame U.S. foreign policy.

*Cheney, Glenn Alan. Revolution in Central America. New
   York: Franklin Watts, 1984. 90 p. ISBN: 0-531-04761-X.
   $10.00. Gr. 7-12.

This is an objective, concise and readable description of

the many serious issues involving the people of Nicaragua, El Salvador, Honduras and Guatemala. Cheney discusses the long-standing historical problems that have affected the area for centuries as well as present-day East-West political struggles between the United States and the Soviet Union. The author is indeed realistic in evaluating the problems and difficult solutions that lie ahead for Central America. His conclusions reflect the tragic state of affairs in Central America today: "The problems in Central America are too deeply rooted in the past and too tightly interconnected with global politics to be corrected by a fleet of ships, and infusion of money, or the good intentions of neutral negotiators. As long as hunger, disease, ignorance, greed, revenge, fear, distrust, and despair remain, the fighting is bound to continue" (p. 86).

Diskin, Martin, ed. Trouble in Our Backyard: Central America and the United States in the Eighties. New York: Pantheon Books 1983. 266 p. ISBN: 0-394-52295-8. $19.50. Gr. 10-adult.

The purpose of these eleven essays is to emphasize the fact that the Reagan administration is definitely wrong in its policies toward Central America. It includes essays on Central America today, the role of religion and specific essays on El Salvador, Nicaragua, Guatemala and Honduras. In addition, it includes a passionate indictment against President Reagan and his government for his policies against the Sandinista government in Nicaragua written by the German novelist Günter Grass. The problems of Central America are so basic, so severe and of such long duration that I wonder if it is fair or just a simplistic solution to blame the United States, as the editor does in the introduction: "The United States can, and probably will, rain death on innocent people in Central America, as it did in Southeast Asia some years ago, but the impulses that Guatemalan Indians, Salvadoran peasants, and Nicaraguan workers are now expressing through their lives and deaths are meaningful" (p. xxxiii).

Jacobsen, Peter, and Preben Kristensen. A Family in Central America. New York: The Bookwright Press, 1986. 32 p. ISBN: 0-531-18081-6. $9.40. Gr. 3-6.

The Figueroas, a poor rural family in Costa Rica, tell about their home, work, food and other interests. Magnificent color photographs of the Figueroa family at work and at play provide young readers with an intimate, touching view in the lives of "a Central American Indian family who live in the remote forests of Costa Rica" (p. 7). Young readers should realize that this book depicts only the life of a very poor family in Costa Rica. It should not be read as a source of information or understanding about life in Costa Rica, much less Central America.

Langley, Lester D. Central America: The Real Stakes. New York: Crown Publisher, Inc., 1985. 280 p. ISBN: 0-517-55706-1. $15.95. Gr. 9-adult.

This is another book, like many that are currently being published, which indicts U.S. foreign policy--past and present--in Central America. The author, a historian, provides a readable guide to Central America's salient features, its politics, its culture and its conflicts. As such, it provides much interesting information on Nicaragua, Honduras, El Salvador, Guatemala and Costa Rica. But, as an in-depth discussion of current U.S. policy in Central America, it leaves much to be desired. It is one naïve man's opinion about how to solve the problems in Central America: "... our place in this future conflict should be outside Central America. From off its shores we can more capably shield the Central Americans from other meddlers, like the Cubans or Soviets, and carry out such a mission with considerably less cost in lives and material than by plunging into mountainous Honduras with an army to protect our 'credibility.' ... Central Americans want no less than nationhood, and they are willing to pay as high a price as we did to achieve it" (p. 261-262). If only the social, political, economic and ideological problems in Central America were so easily resolved.

Lye, Keith. Take a Trip to Central America. (Take a Trip to) New York: Franklin Watts, Inc., 1985. 32 p. ISBN: 0531-10010-3. $9.40. Gr. 3-5.

An easy-to-read text and outstanding photographs in color introduce children to the people, history and customs of

Central America. Briefly and simply, it tells about the
Mayan civilization, the Spanish conquest, the cities, occupations, agricultural products and other aspects of life
in Central America. It is regrettable that on the page,
"Facts about Central America," the capital "Guatamala"
[sic] City is misspelled.

McCuen, Gary E. Political Murder in Central America: Death
Squads & U.S. Policies. (Ideas in Conflict Series) Hudson,
WI: Gary E. McCuen Publications, 1985. 136 p. ISBN:
0-86596-050-X. $10.95. Gr. 9-12.

The purpose of this series is to feature ideas in conflict
on political, social and moral issues by presenting counterpoints, debates, opinions, commentary and analysis. This
volume presents ideas in conflict on the political violence
from the Central American extreme right and extreme left
as well as counterpoints on death squads and U.S. policy,
a debate on the questions of sanctuary for Central American
refugees in the United States and a limited foreign perspective on the Central American conflicts. The extreme positions represented in these readings and the sensational
nature of these selections--detailed descriptions of torture
and terror on innocent victims--do not provide students
with enough background information to be able to analyze
or evaluate the difficult issues involved in Central America.
In addition, the unclear, dark black-and-white photos and
cartoons do not add to the students' understanding of the
problems in Central America today.

*Nuccio, Richard A. What's Wrong, Who's Right in Central
America? A Citizen's Guide. New York: Facts on File
Publications, 1986. 136 p. ISBN: 0-8160-1374-8. $15.95.
Gr. 9-adult.

This is an extraordinarily objective and informative book
on Central America. As stated in the preface, it is
"not written to support or to oppose official policy in Central America. It is designed to provide average citizens
with basic information and analysis that will allow them
to make their own judgments about what U.S. policy in the
region should be" (p. ix). The author, who is director
of the Roosevelt Center for American Policy studies, a

nonpartisan, nonadvocacy institution, should be commended for writing a most complete guide to the many issues surrounding Central America today. It includes brief summaries of the history of the entire Central American region, "snapshots" that update political developments to late 1985 and a guide to the policy debate for each of the five countries told from the perspectives of a "national security analyst" and a "human rights activist." It is very difficult indeed to find a better written, more objective or more complete book about Central America today than this one.

*Rediscovered Masterpieces of Mesoamerica: Mexico--Guatemala --Honduras. Edited by Gerald Berjonneau and Jean-Louis Sonnery. New York: Rizzoli, 1986. 288 p. ISBN: 0-8478-0709-6. $75.00. Gr. 10-adult. (See annotation under "Mexico")

Revolution in Central America. Edited by Stanford Central America Action Network. Boulder, CO: Westview Press, 1983. 508 p. ISBN: 0-86531-540-X. $32.50. Gr. 10-adult.

In a passionate, dogmatic and repetitious manner, the authors of these forty-eight articles on the revolution in Central America corroborate the statements by Richard R. Fagen in the foreword: "the editors of this volume ... have made choices and make no attempt to hide their sympathies. They are for the Nicaraguan Revolution, for the popular movements in the rest of Central America, and against U.S. imperialism" (p. xi). Thus, page after page, the reader is barraged with one-sided views of the problems in Central America with the inevitable conclusion: [Central American countries] "share a common pattern of dependent capitalist development that is a direct consequence of U.S. domination of the region" (p. 1). For readers who share these beliefs, this may be reassuring reading; readers who want an in-depth analysis of the revolution in Central America will need to search elsewhere.

CHILE

*Huber, Alex. We Live in Chile. (Living Here Series) New
York: The Bookwright Press, 1986. 60 p. ISBN: 0-
531-18023-9. $10.90. Gr. 4-8.

Like previous titles in this series, this book includes
twenty-six first person interviews of people from Chile who
describe their lives, occupations, and the area of the country in which they live. Outstanding color photographs
complement the informative two-page interviews. Most of
the people interviewed represent middle-class workers,
such as an archaeologist, astronomer, teacher, wine taster,
farmer's wife, an intrepid female skydiver (Chile's Women's
National Parachute Champion) and others.

Neruda, Pablo. Art of Birds. Illustrated by Jack Unruh.
Translated by Jack Schmitt. Austin: University of Texas
Press, 1985. 87 p. ISBN: 0-292-70371-6. $14.95. Gr.
9-adult.

Chile's Nobel laureate Pablo Neruda first published these
fifty-three short lyrics in Chile in 1966. In them, he cele-
brates the beauty and special characteristics of the birds
of his native land. Unruh's black-and-white illustrations
beautifully capture Neruda's intense feelings for the
variety and charm of his country's birds.

*Neruda, Pablo. One Hundred Love Sonnets/Cien Sonetos de
Amor. Translated by Stephen Tapscott. Austin: University of Texas Press, 1986. 222 p. ISBN: 0-292-7602-0.
$9.95. Gr. 9-adult.

Tapscott, the translator, states that he selected these

poems because, "they represent Neruda's attempt to incorporate this affectionate, earthy, daily surrealist-and-political vision in a 'classical' body, that of the sonnet" (p. vii). And, because of what Neruda might contribute to "our North American tradition, a voice of intelligent sensual joy" (vii). Indeed, these passionate and imaginative poems dedicated to Matilde Urrutia, Neruda's third wife, will move and charm all romantic readers. The able and easy-flowing English translation has maintained the joy and zest of the original poems by the 1971 Nobel prize winner. For example:

> I crave your mouth, your voice, your hair. Silent and starving, I prowl through the streets. Bread does not nourish me, dawn disrupts me, all day I hunt for the liquid measure of your steps....
> ... and I pace around hungry, sniffing the twilight, hunting for you, for your hot heart, like a puma in the barrens of Quitratúe [p. 27].

Neruda, Pablo. The Separate Rose. Translated by William O'Daly. Port Townsend, WA: Copper Canyon Press, 1985. 65 p. ISBN: 0-914742-88-4. $8.00. Gr. 9-adult.

Young readers might enjoy this example of Neruda's late work, which grew out of a trip the Chilean Nobel laureate took to Easter Island in 1971, when he was dying of cancer. The well-done English translation, which faces the Spanish original, reflects Neruda's reconstruction of our prehistoric connection with nature and the price that civilization has paid in alienation and sadness.

St. John, Jetty. A Family in Chile. (Families the World Over) Photographs by José Armando Araneda. Minneapolis: Lerner Publication Company, 1986.

Basic facts about Tonino Fuentes, an eleven-year-old boy who lives with his family in central Chile, are presented in an unexciting text with adequate photographs in color. It describes each member of Tonino's family, their responsibilities, his school and recreational activities. This is a limited, yet realistic, view of one family's life in Chile.

Sullivan, Edward J. Claudio Bravo. New York: Rizzoli
International Publications, 1985. 142 p. ISBN: 0-8478-
0655-3. $45.00. Gr. 10-adult.

Claudio Bravo, a Chilean now living in Morocco, paints
still life, erotic male nudes, landscape, and wrapped
packaged. According to the sympathetic narrative, there
are two aspects of continuing importance in Bravo's work:
classicism and eroticism. Readers interested in this contemporary painter will enjoy the high-quality color plates
and the complimentary, albeit superficial, narrative.

White, Steven F., ed. Poets of Chile: A Bilingual Anthology,
1965-1985. Greensboro, NC: Unicorn Press, 1986. 281 p.
ISBN: 0-87775-179-X. $25.00. Gr. 9-adult.

Twenty poets--eighteen men and two women--of the two
most recent generations of Chilean poets are represented
in this bilingual publication. A brief and informative introduction by Juan Armando Epple provides the neophyte
with an overview of new Chilean poetry. One- or two-
paragraph introductions to the life and work of each poet
will also prove useful to readers unfamiliar with Chile's
contemporary poetry.

Zurita, Raúl. Anteparadise: A Bilingual Edition. Trans-
lated by Jack Schmitt. Berkeley: University of California
Press, 1986. 217 p. ISBN: 0-520-05434-2. $19.95.
Gr. 10-adult.

Few young adults will be interested in the passionate love
that Zurita expressed in his poetry about the beaches
and mountains of his native Chile. English-speaking
admirers of this young Chilean poet will rejoice in the
English translation which includes numerous notes. Perhaps, the best explanation about these poems is offered
in the afterword by the translator: "Anteparaíso can be
read as a creative response, an act of resistance, to the
violence and suffering during and after the 1973 coup
that toppled the democratically elected Allende government" (p. 212).

COLOMBIA

*García Márquez, Gabriel. The Story of a Shipwrecked Sailor.
Translated by Randolph Hogan. New York: Alfred A.
Knopf, 1986. 106 p. ISBN: 0-394-54810-8. $13.95.
Gr. 9-adult.

This is a fluid translation of an excellent journalistic report written in 1955 when García Márquez was a young
reporter in his native Colombia. It narrates the experiences
of a twenty-year-old Colombian seaman, Luis Alejandro
Velasco, who survived ten days on a raft at sea without
food or water. Even though this is not considered a literary masterpiece by the Nobel prize-winning author, it
does expose young adults to his robust writing style.

Jacobsen, Peter, and Preben Kristensen. A Family in Colombia. New York: The Bookwright Press, 1986. 32 p.
ISBN: 0-531-18083-2. $9.40. Gr. 3-6.

Life in rural Colombia is depicted through the Urrego
family. Celmira Urrego is a coffee picker, and Guillermo,
her husband, is a painter and a bricklayer. They tell about
their seven children, home, work, food and other interests. Attractive color photographs show the family at
work around the house and in the fields. Young readers
should realize that this is life among the poor people in
Colombia where, of course, "there is no running water...,
nor is there any electricity. All the water for drinking,
washing and cooking has to be brought up from a well in
the garden" (p. 26). Like many other books about Latin
America, this one only shows life among the very poor.

Labbé, Armand J. Colombia Before Columbus: The People,

Culture, and Ceramic Art of Prehispanic Colombia. New
York: Rizzoli International Publications, 1986. 207 p.
ISBN: 0-8478-0770-3. $19.95. Gr. 10-adult.

Serious students of prehispanic Colombian ceramics will
not be disappointed in this informative and authoritative
work with over 250 outstanding black-and-white and color
photographs. Each chapter introduces the reader to a
major prehispanic Colombian culture area and discusses
its archaeology, ethnohistory and ceramic record. Maps,
graphs, a glossary of terms, a chronological cultural table,
a catalogue of all the art and artifacts illustrated, a bibliography and an index complement this scholarly work.

COSTA RICA

Bird, Leonard. Costa Rica: the Unarmed Democracy. London: Sheppard Press, 1984. 224 p. ISBN: 0-900661-37-2. $15.00. Gr. 9-adult.

This political history of Costa Rica was sponsored by the Northern Friends Peach Board, a Quaker body, which "exists to express the historic testimony of the Society of Friends against all war." It includes chapters on the pre-Columbian history of Costa Rica, the Spanish conquest, the development of a state and political developments up to 1984. But the book's main emphasis is Costa Rica's effort to continue to be "an oasis of unarmed democracy in a region of heavily armed dictatorships."

*Costa Rica in Pictures. (Visual Geography Series) Minneapolis: Lerner Publications Company, 1987. 64 p. ISBN: 0-8225-1805-8. $9.95. Gr. 4-9.

Like other recent titles in this series about Central America --El Salvador in Pictures, Guatemala in Pictures and Honduras in Pictures--this book provides an overview of the land, history, government, people and economy of Costa Rica. It provides the reader with a positive and optimistic view of Costa Rica and its people with statements such as: "For the most part, politics in Costa Rica has been marked by stability, respect for laws, aversion to unlimited presidential power, honest public administrations, and free expression" (p. 26). In addition, it provides a realistic assessment of Costa Rica's economic future. The only undesirable aspect of this informative book is that most of the color and black-and-white photographs show rural or blue-collar workers while disregarding middle-class people and their life-styles.

Jacobsen, Peter Otto, and Preben Sejer Kristensen. <u>A Family</u>
<u>in Central America</u>. New York: The Bookwright Press,
1986. 32 p. ISBN: 0-531-18081-6. $9.40. Gr. 3-6.
(<u>See</u> review under "Central America")

CUBA

Benjamin, Medea, and others. <u>No Free Lunch: Food and
Revolution in Cuba Today</u>. San Francisco: Institute for
Food & Development Policy, 1984. 240 p. ISBN: 0-935
028-18-8. $7.95. Gr. 9-adult.

The authors' purpose in writing this book "was to get
beyond polemics and to investigate firsthand the food
realities in Cuba today ... to study the achievements,
problems, and issues raised by Cuba's agricultural and
food experience" (pp. ix-x). Thus, they report in glowing terms the tremendous accomplishments of the Cuban
revolution: "Cuba has made itself the only country in the
hemisphere without undernourished children" (unpaged).
"The streets of Old Havana are no longer lined with pro-
stitutes. A former slave society with many blacks and a
history of discrimination, Cuba is now the most racially
harmonious society we have ever experienced. The rate
of violent crime is among the lowest in the world.... Il-
literacy has been virtually eliminated.... Health care is
free...," p. 180). The authors are quick to find fault
in United States' policies toward Cuba, but barely mention
Cuba's internal problems, such as an oppressive, unpro-
ductive bureaucracy; corruption; lack of political freedom
and others. One wonders why the authors feel so com-
fortable about openly criticizing the U.S. and its relations
toward Cuba, but feel compelled to constantly compliment
the Cuban Revolution and to be very subtle about dis-
cussing its failures and problems.

Boswell, Thomas D., and James R. Curtis. <u>The Cuban-
American Experience: Culture Images and Perspectives</u>.
Totowa, NJ: Rowman & Allanheld Publishers, 1983. 200 p.
ISBN: 0-86598-116-7. $34.50. Gr. 9-adult.

The authors' purpose in writing this book is to provide a broad, systematic overview that incorporates important aspects about Cuban-Americans. The result is a comprehensive, balanced survey which includes a historical perspective on Cuba, Cuban migration to the U.S., Cuban settlement, the Cuban-American population with individual chapters on Miami, language, religion, the arts, cuisine, family and politics. This is a useful compendium of facts, 1980 census figures and other interesting observations regarding the Cuban-American experience in the U.S.

Bourne, Peter G. Fidel: A Biography of Castro. New York: Dodd, Mead & Company, 1986. 332 p. ISBN: 0-396-08518-0. $18.95. Gr. 9-adult.

The author of this political biography of Fidel Castro states in the preface that for a long time he has been fascinated by Castro, "a man of extreme physical daring, astonishing charisma, a larger-than-life personality, a rare talent for survival, and an audacity and self-confidence to project himself on the world scene in a way that no leader of a country of such modest size and population had ever done before" (x). Hence, it should come as no surprise that the author is extremely critical of the United States and its role in Cuban internal affairs and, at the same time, presents a sympathetic view of Castro, the politician, even though at the end he states that "there can be little doubt that Fidel's consuming desire to achieve the greatest historical stature for himself has led him to neglect people's desperate desire for a higher standard of living. His need for total control and to be completely authoritarian in his rule has often blinded him to the circumstances in which many Cubans have to live" (p. 304). This biography provides quite a bit of information about Castro's early years and political life. It will be a big disappointment, however, to readers interested in Castro's personal life, as it provides only scant references to Castro's early marriage, divorce and other personal relationships.

*Dolan, Edward F., and Margaret M. Scariano. Cuba and the United States: Troubled Neighbors. (Impact Book) New York: Franklin Watts, 1987. 128 p. ISBN: 0-531-10327-7. $11.90. Gr. 7-10.

In a fluid, simple manner, the authors trace the history
of relations between Cuba and the United States from the
Revolutionary War with particular emphasis to the twentieth
century. It includes numerous black-and-white photographs
as well as parenthetical notes which add to the readers'
understanding of complex issues between the two countries .
As a balanced, objective and optimistic report of these
neighbors' relationships, this narrative is hard to beat.

Fidel Castro: Nothing Can Stop the Course of History.
Interview by Jeffrey M. Elliot and Mervyn M. Dymally.
New York: Pathfinder Press, 1986. 258 p. ISBN: 0-
87348-661-7. $7.95. Gr. 9-adult.

In March 1985, Professor Elliot and Congressman Dymally
traveled to Cuba to interview Fidel Castro. The results
were twenty-five hours of taped interviews in which Castro
spoke entirely in Spanish. The translated interview reports Castro's views on U.S.-Cuban relations, the Reagan
administration's foreign policy, Latin America's economic
problems, Africa, Afghanistan as well as a few personal
thoughts. As is to be expected, this is a long, self-
laudatory piece on Castro and Cuba with disparaging re-
marks on the Reagan administration.

Franqui, Carlos. Family Portrait with Fidel: A Memoir.
Translated by Alfred MacAdam. New York: Random House,
1984. 262 p. ISBN: 0-394-53260. $8.95. Gr. 10-adult.

Carlos Franqui, a former Cuban guerrilla, director of
radio and press services throughout the Sierra Maestra
campaign against Batista, and later editor of Revolución,
the first newspaper of Castro's government, reports in
this excellent translation on his disenchantment with Fidel
Castro as a man and as a leader. Franqui's most interesting observations are about Castro's style of governing:
"His style has never really changed. He never calls
meetings to discuss what is to be done or even to find out
what is being done. He improvises and never shares
power" (p. 5). The author also provides amusing sketches
of Raúl Castro, Camilo Cienfuegos, Che Guevara, the Rus-
sians in Cuba and other well-known figures of revolutionary
Cuba. There is no question that Mr. Franqui is unhappy

with the results of the Cuban Revolution under Castro:
"What Fidel has done is to impose on Cuba all the punish-
ments he suffered as a boy in his Jesuit school; censure,
separation of the sexes, discipline, thought control, a
Spartan mentality. He hates culture, liberty, and any
kind of literary or scientific brilliance" (p. 170). Despite
observations such as these, Mr. Franqui does not provide
a family portrait with Fidel, as the title suggests. Castro
remains a distant, elusive character in this political memoir.

Fuentes, Norberto. Hemingway in Cuba. Edited by Larry
  Alson. Translated by Consuelo E. Corwin. Secaucus,
  NJ: Lyle Stuart, 1984. 453 p. ISBN: 0-8184-0346-X.
  $22.50. Gr. 10-adult.

It is difficult to say whether admirers of the great Ernest
Hemingway will be disappointed or enthusiastic about this
study which focuses on the more than twenty years that
the author lived in Cuba. There is enough of Hemingway,
the man and the writer, to provide new insights into his
personal life and habits, especially his cherished home,
Finca Vigía, outside of Havana. On the other hand, it
includes so much propaganda for Fidel Castro and the
Cuban Revolution that has nothing to do with Hemingway,
that one can only surmise its intent. Because it is based
primarily on anecdotal material and interviews, Hemingway
devotees can easily skip some of the numerous sections and
still retain the flavor of Hemingway's life in Cuba. A
great number of black-and-white photos as well as trans-
cripts of letters to and from Hemingway and a detailed
description of the contents of the Hemingway home are
also included.

*Haverstock, Nathan A. Cuba in Pictures. (Visual Geo-
  graphy Series) Minneapolis: Lerner Publications Company,
  1987. 64 p. ISBN: 0-8225-1811-2. $8.95. Gr. 5-10.

In a most objective and concise manner, Haverstock introduces the reader to the land, history, government,
people and economy of Cuba. Like the previous edition,
this updated edition discusses the achievements and the
limitations of the Castro regime. Numerous well-selected
black-and-white and color photographs add immensely to

the narrative. The following is an example of the author's objectivity: "Whatever the eventual judgment of history upon Castro, clearly he has improved some of the conditions for his fellow citizens. Yet the Cuban economy is still dominated by one crop and continues to be shackled to foreign sources of supply and assistance" (p. 63).

Kirk, John M. José Martí, Mentor of the Cuban Nation. Gainesville: University Presses of Florida, 1983. 201 p. ISBN: 0-8130-0736-4. $9.00. Gr. 9-adult.

As stated by the author, the fundamental goal of this study is to provide "a reasonable, clear, and objective overview" of José Martí's socio-political thought through a detailed examination of Martí's Complete Works. This book presents a synthesis of Martí's aspirations concerning the type "of political, social, and economic structures that undoubtedly Martí would have striven to introduce into an independent Cuba" (p. x). The author also states that this work "is expected to arouse controversy, perhaps even more so because it purports to offer an essentially 'neutral' overview of Martí's sociopolitical thought and, therefore, is open to criticism from all sides" (p. x). Students of Cuba's great moralist will be interested in reading about Martí's reforms and his intentions to change Cuba into a "raceless, classless, nonsectarian, and well-educated society" (p. 130) written by a self-appointed admirer.

Martí, José. The Golden Age. Illustrated by Michael Santini. Translated by María Elena Hart and Miguel Maranda. Miami: Milos, Inc., 1984. 231 p. ISBN: Unavailable. $20.00. Gr. 10-adult.

Admirers of the great Cuban patriot, José Martí, will enjoy this translation of the four issues of the The Golden Age, a monthly magazine for Hispanic children, which includes instructive stories, historical articles, essays and poems. In his writings for children, Martí expresses his values and beliefs regarding education. He states: "A boy is born to be a gentleman, a girl to be a mother.... The Golden Age is published so that American boys can know how people lived in America and other lands before as well as how they live now, how they make things of

glass and steel..." (p. 3). "For the girls we will write
in a way that will please them ... to touch the girls' souls
with the things that a hummingbird sees as he wanders
curiously among the flowers..." (p. 4). This is not a
publication for children, but rather a tribute to its author.

Mason, Theodore K. Across the Cactus Curtain: The Story
   of Guantánamo Bay. New York: Dodd, Mead & Company,
   1984. 159 p. ISBN: 0-396-08462-1. $13.95. Gr. 9-12.

Mason wrote this journalistic report while he was assigned
as an Armed Forces television station supervisor at Guantánamo Bay. In it, he describes what it is like to live on
the only U.S. base in Communist territory. He also tells
about the history of the base and about present difficulties
in dealing with Fidel Castro. The appendix includes a concise history of Guantánamo Bay. Devotees of life in the
armed forces may be interested in reading about the boring
yet precarious life in this "restricted facility" where no
one can visit without permission, and "no base personnel
can cross the closed frontier into Cuba" (p. 12). The
five phrases in which Spanish words are used all include
spelling mistakes.

Pérez, Louis A., Jr. Cuba Between Empires, 1878-1902.
   Pittsburgh, PA: University of Pittsburgh Press, 1983.
   490 p. ISBN: 0-8229-3472-8. $32.95. Gr. 10-adult.

The author describes Cuba during the years 1878-1902 in
which the United States "followed a policy that was shrewd,
purposeful, and calculated." He states that U.S. intervention "in 1898 blocked the ascendancy of the Cuban
revolutionary forces and preserved intact the prevailing
social order.... No aspect of Cuban society was spared
in this endeavor. Pro-American political parties were
organized.... And under the auspices of the military
government, an annexationist naturalized American citizen
was elected as Cuba's first president" (p. xviii, xix).
This is a unilateral analysis of what the author believes
are the consequences of American intervention in Cuba's
first revolution.

ECUADOR

Lepthien, Emilie U. Ecuador. (Enchantment of the World)
Chicago: Children's Press, 1986. 128 p. ISBN: 0-516-
02760-3. $19.95. Gr. 4-8.

The geography, history, culture, industries, resources and
people of Ecuador are introduced to young readers through
a readable text and numerous photographs in color. Students will find the last chapter, "Mini-Facts at a Glance,"
useful and informative. It also includes a most complete
index.

EL SALVADOR

Adams, Faith. <u>El Salvador: Beauty Among the Ashes</u>. Minneapolis: Dillon Press, 1986. 135 p. ISBN: 0-87518-309-3. $11.95. Gr. 4-7.

As an excellent piece of political propaganda in support of the Guerrilla movement in El Salvador, this book is hard to beat. Even though the author states in the preface that this book "seeks to give a representative view of life in El Salvador" and that "an attempt was made to present the position of all sides in a fair and straightforward way" (p. 4), she then proceeds with statements such as "The guerrillas want to give land to the farm workers who till the soil, reduce poverty and hunger, and provide better education and health care. This revolutionary group believes that it can improve the quality of life for most Salvadorans" (p. 12). Attractive color photographs of mostly poor and rural people accompany this patronizing introduction to the people, history folklore, social life and customs of El Salvador. Like many books of this type, it emphasizes the life of the poor. (In this case, it devotes four paragraphs to the life of the middle- or upper-class Salvadorans.) In the last chapter the author states: "Many sanctuary refugees feel that they must tell their story to make people in the United States aware of what is happening to their country. The refugees claim that the money the United States sends to El Salvador is used to support an unjust government and military. They ask U.S. citizens to write to Congress and the president and tell them to stop sending money to the government and military in El Salvador" (p. 116). Readers should look elsewhere for an objective introduction to this war-torn Central American country.

Duarte, José Napoleón, with Diana Page. Duarte: My Story.
New York: G. P. Putnam's Sons, 1986. ISBN: 0-399-
13202-3. $18.95. Gr. 9-adult.

This political autobiography of El Salvador's president,
José Napoleón Duarte, provides readers with an inside
view of the politics, intrigue and abuses of power prevalent in Central America. Readers interested in Duarte's
personal life will be thoroughly disappointed. With the
exception of a chapter that describes the family's anguish
regarding the recent kidnapping of his daughter by Marx-
ist guerillas, there is little mention of Duarte's personal
life. On the other hand, it includes quite a bit of detail
about the struggles between the oligarchy and the military,
the real life of political repression and Duarte's passionate
beliefs in democracy for his country: "There will be no
common ground as long as the guerillas believe violence is
the only way they can gain power. There are opportunities
for all political beliefs within the democratic system. The
working class can organize to gain power within a democracy. But, the guerillas, who claim to represent the
workers, seem more interested in attacking Christian Dem-
ocrats than trying to change the unjust structure of our
society" (p. 279).

Haverstock, Nathan A. El Salvador in Pictures. (Visual
Geography Series) Minneapolis: Lerner Publications Company, 1987. 64 p. ISBN: 0-8225-1806-6. $9.95. Gr.
4-9.

Like other recent titles in this series about Central America--
Costa Rica in Pictures, Guatemala in Pictures and Honduras
in Pictures--this book provides an overview of the land,
history, government, people and economy of El Salvador.
An ample supply of black-and-white and color photographs
do an excellent job of portraying El Salvador as "the most
densely populated nation on the mainland of the Americas,
with nearly three times as many people per square mile as
the crowded People's Republic of China" (p. 5). As a
basic introduction to El Salvador, it should be welcomed
by most readers. Its weaknesses, however, are in the
following areas: It barely discusses the internal political
problems of El Salvador today. It suggests a simplistic
solution to El Salvador's economic problems. And it reflects

a pathetic misunderstanding of Latin American people, with generalizations such as: "El Salvador's mestizos are serious, hardworking, and less given to exaggeration in expressing sorrow or joy than some other Central Americans" (p. 38.)

GUATEMALA

*Ashabranner, Brent. Children of the Maya: A Guatemalan Indian Odyssey. Photographs by Paul Conklin. New York: Dodd, Mead & Company, 1986. 97 p. ISBN: 0-396-08786-8. $12.95. Gr. 5-10.

In a direct and touching manner, the author relates the problems that the Mayan Indians have had in Guatemala. He describes some of the atrocities they have recently experienced in their own country, their desperate struggle to survive, and their adaptation to a new life in Indiantown, Florida. Moving personal interviews and stark black-and-white photographs convey to the reader the extreme losses and suffering of these new immigrants. This is a most sympathetic view in support of Central American refugees into the U.S.

*Gallenkamp, Charles. Maya: The Riddle and Discovery of a Lost Civilization. Third rev. ed. New York: Viking Penguin, Inc., 1985. 235 p. ISBN: 0-670-80387-1. $22.95. Gr. 9-adult. (See annotation under "Mexico")

Guatemala, Tyranny on Trial: Testimony of the Permanent People's Tribunal. Edited and translated by Susan Jonas and others. (Contemporary Marxism) San Francisco: Synthesis Publications, 1984. 301 p. ISBN: 0-89935-024-0. $9.95. Gr. 10-adult.

The main purpose of this book, which includes the proceedings of the Permanent People's Tribunal held in Madrid, Spain, in January 1983, "is to expose the harsh truths about the Guatemalan military dictatorship originally

imposed and continuously supported by the U.S. government" (p. v). The editors strongly condemn the U.S.
government for its role in Guatemala and describe "U.S.
counter-insurgency foreign policy as fascist: it demands
the defense of its capital interests by insisting that agents,
such as the Guatemalan dictatorship, imposed naked, terrorist
bourgeois rule to suppress working-class and peasant
struggles" (p. xi). It includes numerous eyewitness testi-
monies given by peasants, revolutionary priests, labor
leaders, former army personnel and others that recount
the massacres and terror unleashed against the indigenous
people by the Guatemalan governments since 1954 and
blames the government of the U.S. for these crimes "because of its determinative interference in the affairs of
Guatemala" (p. 266). This is definitely a leftist view of
U.S. foreign policy in Guatemala with its concomitant conclusions.

Guatemala in Pictures. (Visual Geography Series) Minneapolis: Lerner Publications Company, 1987. 64 p. ISBN:
0-8225-1803-1. $9.95. Gr. 4-9.

Like other recent titles in this series about Central Amer-
ica--Costa Rica in Pictures, El Salvador in Pictures
and Honduras in Pictures--this book provides an overview
of the land, history, government, people and economy of
Guatemala. Carefully selected maps and attractive black-
and-white and color photographs complement the dry but
informative text. It is unfortunate, however, that the
photographs incessantly depict the lives of the poor and
the Indians of Guatemala with the authors' inevitable conclusion: "Besides the country's great natural beauty and
its Mayan treasures, Guatemala offers a rare chance to see
Indian people living much as they have for centuries"
(p. 63.) This is definitely a tourist view of Guatemala.

*Perera, Víctor. Rites: A Guatemalan Boyhood. San Diego:
Harcourt Brace Jovanovich, 1986. 194 p. ISBN: 0-15-
177678-4. $15.95. Gr. 9-adult.

Víctor Perera, a Jew born in Guatemala, recalls his childhood and adolescence in a country that sometimes accepted
him and at other times rejected him because of his Jewish

background. Mature readers will be engrossed in the
life of a sensitive young man who experiences many of the
travails and humiliations of young people everywhere.
Despite the Guatemalan/Jewish background of the author,
this touching memoir includes many of the universal anxieties that many of us experience in our road to maturity.
The last part of this memoir can also be read as an interesting, albeit pathetic, political and sociological portrait of Guatemala in the 1980's, including its violence
and intrigue.

*Steltzer, Ulli. Health in the Guatemalan Highlands. Seattle:
University of Washington Press, 1983. 80 p. ISBN:
0-295-96024-8. $9.95. Gr. 8-12.

The extreme poverty and lack of basic needs of the people
of Chimaltenango in Guatemala are amply demonstrated
through touching black-and-white photographs, poignant
interviews, and a detailed introduction written by the
founder of a general community development program,
Dr. Carroll Behrhorst. Even though the purpose of this
book is to describe the community development program,
which includes nutrition and hygiene classes, a network
of rural extension workers, and a revolving loan fund to
help farmers buy land on a cooperative basis, readers
will be touched by the unfortunate living conditions of the
people in the Guatemalan highlands who have been "op-
pressed and exploited by the Spanish conquistadores and by
more than twenty generations of their descendants" (p.
xii).

HONDURAS

<u>Honduras in Pictures</u>. (Visual Geography Series) Minnea-
polis: Lerner Publications Company, 1987. 64 p. ISBN:
0-8225-1804-X. $9.95. Gr. 4-9.

Like other recent titles in this series about Central
America--<u>Costa Rica in Pictures</u>, <u>El Salvador in Pictures</u>
and <u>Guatemala in Pictures</u>--this book provides an overview
of the land, history, government, people and economy of
Honduras. It includes an ample supply of color and black-
and-white photographs as well as carefully selected maps.
It must be noted, however, that many of the black-and-
white photographs are blurred and unappealing. The
authors should also be criticized for their patronizing and
thoughtless description of the language spoken in Honduras:
"Although there are a few areas where the ancient tongues
of the Indians still prevail, the language of Honduras is
Spanish. The Spanish spoken, however, is not the aris-
tocratic Castilian dialect taught in many North American
classrooms. Honduras Spanish not only drops certain
syllables, but contains many words borrowed from the
Mayan language" (p. 48).

LATIN AMERICA

See also Central America and individual countries.

Blasier, Cole. The Giant's Rival: The U.S.S.R. and Latin
America. Pittsburgh, PA: University of Pittsburgh
Press, 1983. 213 p. ISBN: 0-8229-3486-8. $9.95.
Gr. 10-adult.

This is a readable discussion on Soviet-Latin American
relations based primarily on interviews and research in
Moscow. It emphasizes the political, economic and party
relations between the Soviet Union and Latin America with
an excellent chapter on Cuba ("... Soviet policy toward
Cuba has been a smashing success in political terms [and]
... a resounding failure economically" (p. 127). In addition, it includes nineteen tables (many prepared by Soviet
experts), which clarify important economic and political
aspects between the Soviet Union and Latin America. In
the afterword, the author suggests three rules "for the
United States to follow during political upheavals south of
the border: 1. American authorities should prevent the
U.S.S.R. from acquiring any military bases in the Western
Hemisphere. 2. The United States should not intervene
unilaterally with armed forces in any Latin American country. 3. The United States should not attempt to deter-
mine the political leadership of Latin American countries,
whether by economic or military assistance or political
interference" (p. 158). The author states that his three
rules "may seem negative to some readers" (p. 163). I
do not believe they are negative; they are simply naïve.

Brown, Cynthia, ed. With Friends Like These: The Americas

Watch Report on Human Rights and U.S. Policy in Latin America. New York: Pantheon Books, 1985. 281 p. ISBN: 0-394-72949-8. $9.95. Gr. 10-adult.

The purpose of these essays is to demonstrate how the Reagan administration's human rights policies have failed in Chile, Uruguay, Argentina, El Salvador, Honduras, Nicaragua, Guatemala, Peru and Colombia. They consistently blame the Reagan administration's eagerness to please Latin America's despotic rulers and thus support practices of forced disappearances, torture, arbitrary arrest and cold-blooded execution of prisoners in these countries. In addition, the authors are quick to point out that measures to restrict human rights are justified by the Nicaraguan government "because of the emergency resulting from the U.S.'s sponsored invasion, and where the contras themselves have committed many serious abuses" (p. 242). This is a strong indictment of the Reagan administration by the Americas Watch group.

*The Cambridge Encyclopedia of Latin America and the Caribbean. Edited by Simon Collier, Harold Blakemore, and Thomas E. Skidmore. New York: Cambridge University Press, 1985. 456 p. ISBN: 0-521-26263-1. $39.50. Gr. 8-adult.

The physical environment, economy, peoples, history, politics and society, as well as the culture of Latin America and the Carribbean are presented in a readable, authoritative and comprehensive manner. This is definitely an important reference source about the history, natural conditions, problems of economic development and international affairs of this region of the world. Excellent maps, charts, and photographs add immensely to the well written text. It is interesting to note that most of the fifty contributors are British specialists which introduces a European perspective to what many times are narrowly focused U.S. vs. Latin American issues.

*The Cambridge History of Latin America. Edited by Leslie Bethell. Vol. 1: Colonial Latin America, 645 p. 1984. ISBN: 0-521-23223-6. $65.00; Vol. 2: Colonial Latin America. 922 p. 1984. ISBN: 0-521-2451-6-8. $75.00;

Vol. 3: From Independence to C., 1870. 945 p. 1985.
ISBN: 0-521-23224-4. $80.00; Vol. 4 & 5: Latin America
Circa, 1870 to 1930. 679 p. and 951 p. 1986. $69.50.
(set) ISBN: 0-521-23225-2. New York: Cambridge University Press. Gr. 9-adult.

There is no question that the editor definitely achieved
his purpose in producing a "high-level synthesis of exist-
ing knowledge which will provide historians of Latin
America with a solid base for future research, which students of Latin American history will find useful and which
will be of interest to historians of other areas of the world"
(p. xiv). This is a most readable and authoritative survey
of Latin America's historical experience during almost five
centuries from the first contacts between native American
Indians and Europeans to the present day written by
eminent scholars from the U.S. and abroad. The chronological order of the volumes and the well-organized chapters provide readers with a basic understanding of the
economic, social, political, intellectual and cultural history of Latin America which is almost impossible to find
elsewhere. Informative bibliographical essays are found
at the end of each volume. Volumes 6-8 (Latin America,
1930 to the present) will be published soon.

Carroll, Raymond. The Caribbean: Issues in U.S. Relations.
(Impact Books) New York: Franklin Watts, 1984. 104 p.
ISBN: 0-531-04852-7. $9.90. Gr. 7-12.

This is a brief and concise overview of the people, history,
geography as well as current political, social and economic
developments of the countries in the Caribbean region.
The author does a good job in explaining the colonizations
by Spain, Holland, France and Great Britain. He also
examines, simply yet clearly, the United States "involvement in the Caribbean, highlighting the Monroe Doctrine,
the Cuban missile crisis, Johnson's invasion of the Do-
minican Republic and Reagan's invasion of Grenada.
Carroll seems to be particularly concerned about the potential growth of Marxism-Leninism in the area. He states
that, "where political democracy does not exist in the
Caribbean, the United States hopes to encourage its growth.
Why? For both idealistic and practical reasons. If Americans believe in the value of democracy in the United States

they should wish to see it flourish in every part of the world, and particularly among our Caribbean neighbors" (p. 86).

The Defiant Muse: Hispanic Feminist Poems from the Middle Ages to the Present--A Bilingual Anthology. Edited by Angel Flores and Kate Flores. New York: The Feminist Press, 1986. 149 p. ISBN: 0-935312-54-4. $11.95. Gr. 9-adult. (See annotation under "Spain")

*Galeano, Eduardo. Memory of Fire: Genesis--Part One of a Trilogy. Translated by Cedric Belfrage. New York: Pantheon Books, 1985. 293 p. ISBN: 0-394-54805-1. (V. 1) $17.95. Gr. 9-adult.

Brief historical narratives, based on folklore, history and fiction, poignantly describe mostly Latin American pre-Columbian creation myths and the conquest period of Latin America up to the year 1700. Well-known episodes and people of Latin America's history are recreated in this carefully selected collection of literary sketches. The documentary references used by the author, and listed at the end of the book are an excellent source for further study. This is, indeed, an original form to introduce or supplement the study of Latin America's history for most readers.

Gifford, Douglas. Warriors, Gods & Spirits from Central & South American Mythology. Illustrated by John Sibbick. New York: Schocken Books, 1983. 132 p. ISBN: 0-88894-386-5. $15.95. Gr. 6-12.

Fifty-six myths and legends from Mexico, Central and South America are recounted in this collection which includes both pre-Columbian myths and legends as well as myths "collected in modern times by more scientific and less prejudiced methods" (p. 12). Readers will find legends from the Aztecs, Mayas, Incas, Amazon Region, Paraguay, Argentina and from the people of the far south, which tell about heroes, villains, gods, spirits, magic, animals and rebirth. Eighteen bizarre watercolors and numerous black-and-white line drawings provide stylized,

symbolic decoration to the oftentimes dull text. Unfortunately, many of these legends and myths are only available in Spanish--hence, many English readers will need
to refer to this anthology until there are better versions
available in English for young readers.

Griffiths, John. The Caribbean in the Twentieth Century.
(Twentieth Century World History) North Pomfret, VT:
Batsford, distr. by David & Charles. 1984. 72 p.
ISBN: 0-7134-3839-8. $14.95. Gr. 7-12.

In a strong anti-U.S. and pro-Cuban attitude, Griffiths
traces the history of the Caribbean countries from the
end of the nineteenth century to the present day. He
emphasizes United States' "abuses" in several of the
Caribbean countries and is also critical of the role that
the British government has had in intending "to perpetuate
its control over the West Indies" (p. 19). The author
has nothing but kind words to say about Castro's Cuba;
such as: "The achievements of the Cuban Revolution in
health, education, housing, employment and welfare
provision have made Cuba a model for development in the
Caribbean, since it has dealt definitely with the problems
which still plague the rest of the area" (p. 40). Con-
versely, he blames the United States for saturating the
Caribbean with U.S. culture, for using force when necessary to support its control of the region and for "using
cruder techniques, such as assassinations, in its attempts
to destabilize governments and manipulate the affairs of
countries, as many attempts on the life of Fidel Castro
throughout the 1960s, and probably beyond, have shown"
(p. 55.) The text-book-like questions at the end of each
chapter and the author's unconcealed distaste for anything
American are two obvious reasons why readers might prefer other books on the Caribbean.

*Handbook of Latin American Popular Culture. Edited by
Harold E. Hinds and Charles M. Tatum. Westport, CT:
Greenwood Press, 1985. 259 p. ISBN: 0-313-23293-8.
$45.00. Gr. 9-adult.

Readers interested in a basic overview to ten areas of
popular culture in Latin America--popular music, popular

religion, comics, television, sport, photonovels, film, festivals and carnivals, the single-panel cartoon and newspapers--will be delighted with this handbook. Each chapter gives a history of the subject, followed by sections that describe specific historical and current sources of information and concludes with discussions of research collections, future directions for research and bibliographies listing all the works cited. The serious lack of basic research tools such as bibliographies, collections, guides to collections, catalogues, descriptive surveys and monographic studies makes this an excellent starting point for the study of Latin American popular culture.

Highwater, Jamake. Native Land: Sagas of the Indian Americas. Boston: Little, Brown and Company, 1986. 230 p. ISBN: 0-316-3687-2. $24.95. Gr. 9-adult.

Highwater wrote this book to elaborate upon the original public television program series on the cultural history of pre-Columbian American civilizations. It includes chapters on the Olmecs, Mayas, Incas and Aztecs as well as the Mound Builders and Cliff Dwellers and the warriors of the great Plains. Readers interested in an overview of these great cultures will appreciate Highwater's readable narrative. Numerous, although not particularly good, black-and-white photographs illustrate each chapter.

*Hopkins, Jack W., ed. Latin America: Perspectives on a Region. New York: Holmes & Meier Publishers, Inc., 1987. 320 p. ISBN: 0-8419-0917-2. $39.50. Gr. 9-adult.

This collection of eighteen essays introduces the reader to Latin America from the perspective of twenty-two contributors. It is divided into three parts--background, foundations of development and contemporary dimensions --with individual chapters on the environment, history, religion, education, politics, literature and other aspects of Latin American life and culture. In a direct and most approachable manner, each chapter provides a thorough discussion of particular subjects which can be searched for specific information or for a more general understanding of Latin America as a whole. Notes and suggested readings are included at the end of each chapter.

Karlowich, Robert A. Rise Up in Anger: Latin America
Today. New York: Julian Messner, 1985. 175 p. ISBN:
0-671-46525-2. $9.29. Gr. 8-12.

A more suitable title for this book is The Worst of Central
and South America: Corruption, Assassinations and
Poverty. There is no question that, to a greater or
lesser degree, as stated by the author, "Latin America
remains largely economically depressed; suffers from
widespread social and economic inequality, extreme poverty, and authoritarian traditions; and continues under
foreign economic control and political influence" (p. 21).
But, to devote a whole book to Latin America today, and
ignore Mexico and Costa Rica because they "have relatively
stable governments" (p. 23) and then indict the rest of
Central and South America for their corruption and constant assassinations; the United States for its undue influence in the region; and conclude that "It is time the
Latin Americans were allowed to find their own paths
in the world. It is time they were allowed to reconcile
their internal forces in a manner all the people deem
best for themselves. It is time they received back from
those nations who have ignored or misused them in the
past a sympathetic and honest helping hand toward the
realization of their own goals" (p. 167) is indeed simplistic.
These are empty political platitudes appropriately illustrated with numerous black-and-white photos of dismal
slum and rural scenes of South and Central America.
There is too much beauty and vitality in Latin America
today that this author does not see or chooses to ignore.

*Love Poems from Spain and Spanish America. Selected
and Translated by Perry Higman. San Francisco: City
Lights Books, 1986. 243 p. ISBN: 0-87286-183-X.
$7.95. Gr. 8-adult. (See annotation under "Spain")

*Osborne, Harold. South American Mythology. [Rev. ed.]
(Library of the World's Myths and Legends) New York:
Peter Bedrick Books, 1986. 144 p. ISBN: 0-600-34281-6.
$18.95. Gr. 9-adult.

The objective of this book is to present a sample of what
is known about the mythological South America. Thus,

in a large-format volume with spectacular color and black-and-white photos, it describes the myths, legends and folklore of the Inca, Collao, Chibcha, Araucanian and other South American pre-Columbian civilizations. Serious students of this genre will find this book interesting and appealing.

Paz, Octavio. One Earth, Four or Five Worlds: Reflections on Contemporary History. Translated by Helen R. Lane. New York: Harcourt Brace Jovanovich, Publishers, 1985. 213 p. ISBN: 0-15-169394-3. $14.95. Gr. 10-adult.

Octavio Paz, one of Mexico's foremost intellectuals, is also a diplomat, political analyst, writer, anthropologist, philosopher and poet. In these articles and essays, he expresses his personal views about the contemporary scene. He discusses Europe's problems with prosperity, the United States' position as an "imperial democracy," the Soviet Union's totalitarian empire, the dilemmas of the Third World and Latin America's monumental economic and political problems. Mr. Paz's honest and straightforward observations about Latin America's unresolved issues are refreshingly candid. The following are his assertions regarding Mexico's economic crisis of 1982: "The country was--and still is--confronted with a disastrous economic situation. The causes are well known: the deterioration of the worldwide economy...; the rash and improvident policies of the Mexican government, which once again turned a deaf ear to those of us who had repeatedly expressed our concern about the careless way in which the tremendous wealth from the newly discovered oil deposits was being handled: and the endemic disease of patrimonialist regimes such as the Mexican: the corruption and venality of government of officials" (p. 123). About Cuba, he states: "the Cubans today are as poor as or poorer than they were before, and far less free; inequality has not disappeared: the hierarchies are different, and yet they are not less rigid but more rigid and draconian; repression is like the island's heat: continuous intense, and inescapable; it continues to be economically dependent on sugar, and politically dependent on the Soviet Union" (p. 187).

Randall, Margaret. Women Brave in the Face of Danger:

Photographs of and Writings by Latin and North American Woman. Trumansburg, NY: The Crossing Press, 1985. [126 p.] ISBN: 0-89594-161-9. $10.95. Gr. 9-adult.

Sensuous, emotional black-and-white photographs of poor women from Latin America as well as middle-class and working American women combined with passionate writings (verse and prose) about human suffering, Nicaraguan politics, the Cuban revolution, lesbian love, rape and motherhood give this collection a special feminine meaning to the concept of bravery. This is a forceful political/ feminist statement that will arouse strong emotions in all readers and viewers.

Reader's Digest. Mysteries of the Ancient Americas. Pleasantville, NY: The Reader's Digest Association, Inc., 1986. 320 p. ISBN: 0-89577-183-7. $25.95. Gr. 8-adult.

Numerous color photographs and drawings of ancient America are the most appealing part of this book. And this may be the only reason for selecting this book for readers of any age. The text pretends to interest readers in the mysteries that have intrigued historians, archaeologists and laymen about pre-Hispanic civilizations. The results are a series of wild speculations, romanticized versions, unsubstantiated theories, such as: "According to him, [Erich von Daniken] not only culture, but the race of man was engineered as the result of visits from ancient astronauts" (p. 20) as well as serious historical descriptions of the new world before Columbus. If the purpose is only to interest readers in ancient America, this attractive volume may, perhaps, serve a function. Otherwise, there are many better historial books, at all levels of sophistication, which describe ancient America from a less confusing and more academic perspective.

Troughton, Joanna, retel. How the Birds Changed Their Feathers. (Folktales of the World) Illustrated by the author. New York: Bedrick/Blackie, 1986. 32 p. ISBN: 0-216-90084-0. $10.95. Gr. K-2.

This tale, told by the Arawak people of Guyana and other South American tribes, tells how the birds, who were

once entirely white, became brightly colored. Primitive
style illustrations, vivid watercolors and a direct, fast-
moving text combine to make this retelling of a popular
tale an enjoyable reading experience.

Weiss, Ann E. Good Neighbors? The United States and
Latin America. Boston: Houghton Mifflin Company, 1985.
148 p. ISBN: 395-36316-0. $12.95. Gr. 6-9.

It is definitely not easy to give clear and simple explanations of the many factors--historical, economic and politi-
cal--that surround the turbulent relationships between
the U.S. and Latin America. And this book is a vivid
testimony to the dangers inherent in trying to give simple
answers to complex and difficult questions. In an easy-
to-read journalistic style, the author attempts to explain
the differences between the U.S. and Latin America from
both the U.S. and the Latin American perspectives. Due
to the incomparable freedom of the press in the U.S.,
there is much published evidence that seems to condemn
the U.S. for taking advantage of its southern neighbors.
And, like many other recent books on Central America,
this book also is highly critical of the U.S. foreign policy
and insists that the U.S. ought to help Latin America "do
all it can to eliminate the social and economic problems
that help give communism its appeal" (p. 124).

Weiss, Jaqueline Schachter, col. & adapt. Young Brer
Rabbit and Other Trickster Tales from the Americas.
Illustrated by Clinton Arrowood. Owing Mills, Maryland:
Stemmer House Publishers, 1985. 65 p. ISBN: 0-88045-
037-1. $14.95. Gr. 4-6.

This collection of fifteen trickster tales from Venezuela,
Brazil, Panama, Martinique, Puerto Rico and Colombia will
remind American readers of the Brer Rabbit stories. And
this is unfortunate. The original tales, as told in Central
and South America, are not imitations of the American Brer
Rabbit stories, but amusing, lively versions of Tío Conejo
(Uncle Rabbit) constantly outsmarting his "friend" and
enemies. A few of the tales are entertaining and fun;
others, however, are bland imitations of the American
tales. The color and black-and-white illustrations are
the most enjoyable aspect of this collection.

Alemán Velasco, Miguel. Copilli: Aztec Prince. New York:
Doubleday & Co., Inc., 1984. 129 p. ISBN: 0-385-
18901-X. $8.50. Gr. 10-adult.

The triumphs and travails of a young Aztec prince,
Copilli, are narrated in what has been called a "novel,
historical narrative and autobiography combined." Inspired by a Florentine Codex, the author has created
Copilli's tale, including particularly the supernatural influences on his life. Thus, the events recorded consti-
tute "the life, reflections, doctrine and predictions of a
young son of the historical ruler Axayácatl" (xi). This
is an intense, imaginative view of Aztec society which may
be of interest to those readers versed in the subject.
It is difficult reading, however, for young readers unfamiliar with Aztec customs and beliefs.

Beezley, William H. Judas at the Jockey Club and Other
Episodes of Porfirian Mexico. Lincoln: University of
Nebraska Press, 1987. 181 p. ISBN: 0-8032-1195-3.
$19.95. Gr. 10-adult.

The lives of everyday Mexicans in the late nineteenth
century are described through anecdotes, folk humor,
sports, travelers' accounts and other sources in this well-
documented historical narrative. It includes foreigners'
descriptions of the way Mexican people during Porfirian
times participated in recreational activities such as bullfighting, baseball, bicycling and rejected modern tech-
nology in their cooking habits, household and agricultural
implements. Some readers might object to what appear
to be strictly Protestant, Anglo-American observations of

"Mexican backwardness" which is viewed as "stagnant, ancient or primitive." Others will delight in this example of well-written social history.

Bethancourt, T. Ernesto. The Great Computer Dating Caper. New York: Crown Publishers, Inc., 1984. 146 p. ISBN: 0-517-55213-2. $10.95. Gr. 8-12.

Eddie Ramirez, an eighteen-year-old high school senior, is eager to help his father, Cisco, who, thus far, has failed in numerous attempts to get rich quickly. Eddie and his close friend, Jody, set up a computer-dating service which provides the money for Cisco to launch his latest invention: a carburetor that allows cars with V-8 engines to get forty m.p.g. Even though, initially, everything seems to go as planned, the computer-dating service is a financial success and Cisco's carburetor does work, they are soon confronted by big problems. The boys are accused of running a teenage sex-for-profit ring and Cisco is threatened with lawsuits by the three big car manufacturers. There are many fashionable ingredients in this novel: a computer whiz kid; a happy-go-lucky Mexican adult, who was a "terrific mariachi"; a refined, well-educated Spanish grandfather who, despite his formality, saved his family in times of trouble, and; unfortunately, weak, insecure and terribly dependent female characters.

Bethancourt, T. Ernesto. The Me Inside of Me. Minneapolis: Lerner Publications Company, 1985. 155 p. ISBN: 0-8225-0728-5. $10.95. Gr. 7-10.

Alfredo (Freddie) Flores, a seventeen-year-old who grew up in a middle-class Mexican-American neighborhood in Santa Amelia, is suddenly rich after his whole family died in an airplane crash. This fast-paced novel centers on Freddie's adjustment to unexpected wealth with strong doses of didactic messages to young adults: the evils of dope, the benefits of education and the problems of U.S. born Mexican-Americans in a prejudiced society. The novel lacks honest characters, yet thrives on action to maintain readers' interests. In addition to the contrived incidents in the novel, readers should realize that the Spanish language is genuinely butchered almost every time it is used

by either Latino or Anglo characters who supposedly
"speak Spanish, and well."

*Bierhorst, John, retel. Doctor Coyote: A Native American
Aesop's Fables. Illustrated by Wendy Watson. New York:
The MacMillan Publishing Company, 1987. [46 p.] ISBN:
0-02-409780-3. $14.95. Gr. 3-5.

These twenty Aztec Aesop's fables were adapted by Indian
retellers in the 1500s. In this English retelling by the
well-known translator of Aztec and American Indian literature, John Bierhorst, the fables have a distinct Aztec
flavor including the characters, Coyote and Puma, and
native figures of speech, such as "those words come back
to bite him." The soft pastel watercolor illustrations which
face each page of text convey the essence of each fable.

*Bierhorst, John, ed. The Hungry Woman: Myths and
Legends of the Aztecs. New York: William Morrow and
Company, 1984. 148 p. ISBN: 0-688-02766-0. $10.25.
Gr. 9-adult.

Twenty-seven Aztec myths and legends that vividly recount the Aztec civilization, as viewed by the Aztecs
themselves, are included in this book. It includes creation
myths about the fall of Tula, the founding of Mexico, in
the days of Montezuma and after Cortes. A few black-and-
white illustrations by Aztec artists of the Sixteenth Century
taken from the Florentine Codex add a sense of realism to
these myths and legends. A very well-written introduction
complements this collection of authentic Aztec literature.

Bierhorst, John, ed. The Monkey's Haircut and Other Stories
Told by the Maya. Illustrated by Robert Andrew Parker.
New York: William Morrow and Company, 1986. 152 p.
ISBN: 0-688-04169-4. $13.00. Gr. 4-8.

Collection of twenty-two Maya folktales that includes myths
of the gods, just-so-stories, witch stories and animal trickster tales. Teachers and librarians will find the lengthy
introduction most informative and an excellent complement
to the study of the Maya. It explains what a Maya house

looks like, what foods are eaten, how a cornfield is planted, what gods are worshipped and what troubles a young man may have with his bride's parents. Young readers will be more apt to enjoy these tales if they have some background to Mayan customs and beliefs. Two-tone, line-and-wash drawings enhance some of the tales.

*Bierhorst, John, translator. Spirit Child: A Story of the Nativity. Illustrated by Barbara Cooney. New York: William Morrow and Company, 1984. [32 p.] ISBN: 0-688-02609-5. $11.50. Gr. 3-6.

The story of the nativity as told by the Aztecs is exquisitely presented in this beautifully illustrated book. The Aztec culture and the Christian religion are honestly depicted in the carefully translated text and in the stunning pre-Columbian-style illustrations. This is definitely a joyous introduction to the Aztecs as well as a message of hope through the spirit child.

*Blackmore, Vivien, adapt. Why Corn Is Golden: Stories About Plants. Illustrated by Susana Martínez-Ostos. 46 p. ISBN: 0-316-54820-0.

*de Gerez, Toni, adapt. My Song Is a Piece of Jade: Poems of Ancient Mexico in English and Spanish. Illustrated by William Stark. 45 p. ISBN: 0-316-81088-6.

*Hinojosa, Franciso, adapt. The Old Lady Who Ate People: Frightening Stories. Illustrated by Leonel Maciel. 47 p. ISBN: 0-316-54220-2.

*Kurtycz, Marcos and Ana García Kobeh, adapt. Tigers and Oppossums: Animal Legends. Illustrated by the authors. 45 p. ISBN: 0-316-50718-0.
Ea. Vol.: Boston: Little Brown & Co., 1984. $12.95. Gr. 5-10.

The striking colorful illustrations and beautiful presentations are indeed appropriate in this outstanding series of

Mexican legends, poems and folktales. All text is in
English, with the exception of the Toltec poems, My Song
Is a Piece of Jade which is in both English and Spanish.
Why Corn Is Golden is a collection of six Mexican pre-
Columbian legends about plants, flowers and fruits that
should appeal to most readers. My Song Is a Piece of
Jade is an excellent introduction to pre-Columbian culture,
gods, and literature through Nahuatl poems. The Old
Lady Who Ate People includes four Mexican legends of
spirits and phantoms. And Tigers and Oppossums is an
excellent adaptation of six Mexican legends about animals
that will charm readers with their wit and resourcefulness.

Brenner, Leah. An Artist Grows Up in Mexico: Scenes from
the Boyhood of Diego Rivera. Illustrated by Diego Rivera.
Albuquerque: The University of New Mexico Press, 1987.
134 p. ISBN: 0-8263-0924-0. $8.95. Gr. 7-adult.

Diego Rivera told these seven stories to his secretary,
Leah Brenner, in the 1930's. In them, he recalls episodes
of his early years in prerevolutionary Mexico and adds a
blend of fantasy and the supernatural. Admirers of the
great Mexican artist will enjoy these stories that provide
amusing glimpses in the life of a unique personality. In
addition, Rivera's black-and-white line illustrations add a
personal touch to each story.

Casagrande, Louis B., and Sylvia A. Johnson. Focus on
Mexico: Modern Life in an Ancient Land. Photographs
by Phillip Bournes. Minneapolis: Lerner Publications
Company, 1986. 96 p. ISBN: 0-8225-0645-9. $9.95.
Gr. 6-9.

This is a poorly organized book which attempts to provide
a history of Mexico, an overview of life in modern Mexico
and an introduction to four young Mexicans of different
socioeconomic backgrounds. The chapter on the history
of Mexico includes many simplistic assertions and vague
generalities which will, at best, confuse young readers
unfamiliar with Mexico's troubled history. Interspersed
in the chapters on four young Mexicans, the authors have
included much valuable and realistic information on modern
Mexico. Unfortunately, young readers have to plod through

sixty pages to acquire glimpses of Mexico's present economic and social problems. An ample supply of black-and-
white and some color photographs add interest to the sometimes wordy narrative.

*Casasola, Agustín Víctor. ¡Tierra y Libertad! Photographs
of Mexico, 1900-1935. New York: Universe Books, 1986.
104 p. ISBN: 0-87633-981-4. $14.95. Gr. 8-adult.

The many faces of the men and women of Mexico who
struggled and lived the Mexican Revolution are artistically
and sensitively portrayed in these one hundred and fifty
black-and-white prints from the Casasola Archive. As
stated in the introduction, Casasola's work "today forms
the richest photographic testimony of the revolutionary
armed struggle of Mexico's social and political life, and
of the role of the people in the building of contemporary
Mexico" (p. 6). There is no question that these photographs will increase the viewers' understanding of Mexico
and its people from the years 1910 until 1935.

Cisneros, Sandra. The House on Mango Street. Houston:
Arte Público Press, 1985. 102 p. ISBN: 0-934770-20.
$7.50. Gr. 5-9.

In a series of brief chapters, a young Mexican-American
girl, Esperanza, records her feeling about the sad world
around. The house on Mango Street is an old, dilapidated
house with one bathroom and one bedroom that she has to
share with her mama, papa, two brothers and one sister.
The cheerless surroundings and the pathetic living conditions, especially of the women in her neighborhood,
depict a hard and almost hopeless existence.

*Cox, Beverly J., and Anderson, Denna Jones. Miguel
Covarrubias Caricatures. Washington, DC: Smithsonian
Institution Press, 1985. 163 p. ISBN: 0-87474-340-0.
$24.95. Gr. 9-adult.

Miguel Covarrubias was only eighteen years old when he
arrived in New York City in 1923. In less than three
years, he became America's most highly acclaimed

caricaturist. This fascinating book includes eighty-four of Covarrubias' finest caricatures which were selected for an exhibition at the National Portrait Gallery. Each illustration is annotated with the subject's dates, an explanation of who he or she is, and quotations from a commentator or from the text that accompanied the drawing's original publication. This is indeed a glorious tribute to one of New York's foremost satiric artists and his great ability to capture the essence of the prominent people of his day.

*Diego Rivera: A Retrospective. New York: W. W. Norton and Company, 1986. 372 p. ISBN: 0-393-02275-7. $60.00. Gr. 9-adult.

The Instituto Nacional de Bellas Artes and the Detroit Institute of Arts collaborated to produce this outstanding catalogue which provides a comprehensive overview of Rivera's life and work and also addresses major aspects of the career of this renowned Mexican artist. Serious students of Rivera's artistic production as well as neophytes will delight in the numerous family photographs and beautiful prints and photographs of Rivera's paintings and murals. The ten scholarly essays provide further testimony to Rivera's artistic accomplishments.

*Espejel, Carlos, and others. The Nelson A. Rockefeller Collection of Mexican Folk Art: A Gift to the Mexican Museum. San Francisco: Chronicle Books, 1986. 79 p. ISBN: 0-87701-446-9. $14.95. Gr. 9-adult.

Through outstanding black-and-white and color photographs and a concise text, the reader/viewer is introduced to the folk art of Mexico. This catalogue includes the most beautiful of the objects donated by the Nelson A. Rockefeller Collection of Mexican Folk Art to the Mexican Museum in San Francisco. It contains toys, ritual objects, ceramics, glassware, lacquerware and clothing.

Favela, Ramón. Diego Rivera: The Cubist years. Phoenix, AZ: Phoenix Art Museum, 1984. 1976 p. ISBN: 0-910407-11-8. $30.00 Gr. 10-adult.

This exhibition catalog includes black-and-white illustrations and color plates of Diego Rivera's Cubist and pre-Cubist works, the majority of which were completed during the painter's stay in Paris between 1909 and 1921. Although serious students of Mexican art will be impressed by this study of Rivera's Cubist period, most readers will be turned off by Favela's affected and unnecessarily pompous writing style. As a study in the evolution of modern Mexican painting, this may serve a useful purpose. It is not, however, an illuminating nor insightful introduction to the works of Diego Rivera.

Fincher, E. B. Mexico and the United States: Their Linked Destinies. New York: Thomas Y. Crowell Co, 1983. 213 p. ISBN: 0-690-04310-4. $11.25. Gr. 6-12.

The main focus of this book are the current problems that affect day-to-day relations between Mexico and the U.S. To explain how these problems developed, the author reviews Mexican history, with particular reference to the influence the U.S. has exerted in the affairs of its neighbor. The author rightfully stresses the continued entry of millions of legal and illegal aliens from Mexico as well as Mexico's weak economy with its concomitant effects. This is an easy-to-understand account of Mexico's ongoing problems with the U.S. with current information as viewed by both American and Mexican scholars, historians and politicians.

Fuentes, Carlos. The Old Gringo. Translated by Margaret Sayers Peden and the author. New York: Farrar, Straus & Giroux, 1985. 199 p. ISBN: 0-374-22578-8. $14.95. Gr. 10-adult.

Revolutionary Mexico is the setting for this intense novel about the American writer Ambrose Bierce, aged 72, who crossed the U.S. Mexican border at El Paso and vanished. Explicit sex and excessive psychologizing are not the correct ingredients to convince the reader of the novel's message: that Mexico's only reality is its "stubborn determination never to be anything other than its eternal, miserable, chaotic self." Nor the novel's heroine, Harriet Winslow, a thirty-one-year-old American, who had the

solution to Mexico's problems: "Look at them, what
these people need is education, not rifles. A good scrub-
bing, followed by a few lessons on how we do things in
the United States, and you'd see an end to this chaos"
(p. 41). Young adults should be exposed to the author--
the well-known Mexican writer Carlos Fuentes--through
his essays or tales; otherwise, they will be disappointed.

*Gallenkamp, Charles. Maya: The Riddle and Discovery of
a Lost Civilization. Third rev. ed. New York: Viking
Penguin, Inc., 1985. 235 p. ISBN: 0-670-80387-1.
$22.95. Gr. 9-adult.

This third revised edition is a most readable and well-
documented history of the Mayas, their obscure origins,
remarkable artistic and intellectual achievements, social
structure and mysterious decline. It incorporates recent
investigations and new information which have become
available since the first edition was published in 1959.
Serious students and general readers will be fascinated by
this vivid reconstruction of "the most brilliant civilization
ever known in pre-Columbian America." No reader will
fail to be impressed by the Maya which "emerged from
shadowy origins to begin a steady climb toward what
eventually became a civilization characterized by monumental architecture, superlative works of art, thriving
trade networks, a system of writing and mathematics, a
highly accurate calendar, a substantial body of astrological
knowledge, and a powerful elite class who ruled over huge
cities--all of which comprised one of the most original
expressions of human ingenuity ever known" (p. 2).
Regrettably, the small, albeit numerous, black-and-white
photographs lack the vitality of the narrative.

Harris, Nathaniel. Montezuma and the Aztecs. Illustrated
by Gerry Wood. (Life and Times) New York: The Bookwright Press, 1986. 60 p. ISBN: 0-531-18028-X. $10.90.
Gr. 4-8.

This is definitely a deplorable introduction to Montezuma
and the Aztec people of pre-Columbian Mexico. The garish
illustrations in full color are grotesque caricatures of the
Aztecs and their way of life. The patronizing, simplistic

text ridicules Aztec culture and beliefs. (For example:
"An Aztec book was a colorful jumble of pictures which
told a story" (p. 4). And the ever-present emphasis on
the Aztec's practice of human sacrifice is insensitive as
well as bizarre: "The Aztecs horrify us just because they
took their beliefs so seriously" (p. 45). In addition, the
author should realize that the Aztecs lived in Mexico, which
is part of North America--not Central America as he repeatedly states. The Aztecs and Montezuma do not deserve
this unenlightened, callous "story."

*Irizarry, Carmen. Passport to Mexico. (Passport to Series)
New York: Franklin Watts, 1987. 48 p. ISBN: 0-531-
10271-8. $11.40. Gr. 4-8.

This is a most comprehensive and informative overview of
Mexico and its people. A direct and easy-to-read narrative,
numerous photographs in color and well-conceived charts
and maps provide the reader with a basic introduction to
Mexico's geography, economy, and life-style. Perhaps,
one could object to the author's positive descriptions of
several aspects of Mexican life. For example, she comments on Mexico's "free and open press" which, she states,
"enjoys great freedom of expression and debates national
and international issues in a lively and forthright manner"
(p. 24). Many of Mexico's leading intellectuals will smile
at such a rosy description of Mexico's press. Despite a
few minor much too optimistic reports on Mexico, this will
provide readers with an attractive and well-balanced view
of Mexico today.

Knowlton, Mary Lee, and Mark J. Sachner, eds. Mexico.
(Children of the World) Photographs by Yoshiyuki Ikuhara.
Milwaukee: Gareth Stevens Publishing, 1987. 64 p. ISBN:
1-55532-161-5. $12.45. Gr. 3-5.

This is definitely the wrong book to introduce children
to Mexico. The one thing that seems to have impressed
the editors is Mexico's poverty. Hence, on almost every
page there is a reference to Mexico's poor people, for
example: "Mexicans do not often go to the dentist even
when they have a toothache, in part because so many of
them are very poor" (p. 21). "Some families are so poor

that the children must go to work right after primary
school" (p. 28). Neither the beauty, nor variety, nor
joy of Mexico and its people are conveyed in this one-sided
view of Mexico.

Jacobsen, Peter O., and Preben S. Kristensen. A Family in
Mexico. New York: Franklin Watts, Inc., The Bookwright
Press, 1984. 32 p. ISBN: 0-531-03787-8. $8.90. Gr.
3-4.

Through the Marmalejo family, the reader is exposed to
life in Mexico City. Each member of the family talks about
his/her interests and hobbies: Mr. Marmalejo, a silver-
smith, explains how he works the metal into beautiful objects. Mrs. Marmalejo, a housewife, is deeply interested
in strengthening the ties in Mexican families. José, a
teenager, goes to school and loves sports and little Mariana
is still shy about her future. In contrast to many books
about Mexico, this one does an outstanding job of portraying the life of a middle-class family in Mexico City without
the common stereotypes and misconceptions. Realistic color
photographs further convey the life-style of many Mexicans
which is often ignored in many books for young readers.
There is only one unfortunate spelling mistake, "Zocala"
[sic], (p. 10, 32), in this otherwise informative and
attractive book about one Mexican family.

Kitchen, Margaret. Grandmother Goes Up the Mountain and
Other Mexican Stories. Illustrated by David Pike. London:
André Deutsch Limited, 1985. 147 p. ISBN: 0-133-97749-X.
$11.00. Gr. 4-6.

Pepita, an eight-year-old girl who lives in Tepingo, a
small village in Mexico, is the only memorable character
in this collection of four stories about rural Mexico. Like
many stories of this type, this one presents life in a Mexican village from the point of view of a foreign tourist.
There are the incessant tortillas and beans and, instead of
a donkey, Pepita's family owns a cow. To add excitement
to these stories, the author has included traditional festivals,
carnivals, and obviously some archaeological treasures. To
add authenticity to a tourist's perspective, "an American
woman, a tourist on holiday in their country" gave the
children ten pesos so that they could go on a ride which

otherwise, Pepita and her brother, Antonio, could not afford. Neither the flat black-and-white line illustrations nor the contrived stories about life in a poor Mexican village offer much for the enjoyment or enlightenment of young readers anywhere.

Littwin, Mike. Fernando Valenzuela, the Screwball Artist. Chicago: Children's Press, 1983. 46 p. ISBN: 0-516-04331-5. $5.95. Gr. 2-4.

An easy-to-read text and dynamic, black-and-white photographs tell the story of Fernando Valenzuela, who is described as one of the best pitchers in the world. It includes well-known facts about Fernando's life with a touch of humor and sincerity, such as: "The Dodger players did not know what to think about Fernando. He weighs more than he should. He does not throw the ball that hard. He does not speak English. And no one could believe he was so young" (p. 28). And yet, "... 'a player like Fernando comes along only once every 15 years'" (p. 22). Young baseball lovers and admirers of Fernando Valenzuela will enjoy this brief biography.

*Litvak King, Jaime. Ancient Mexico: An Overview. Albuquerque: University of New Mexico Press, 1985. 134 p. ISBN: 0-8263-0817-1. $6.95. Gr. 8-adult.

Jaime Litvak King, director of the Institute of Archeological Investigations at the National Autonomous University of Mexico, is eminently qualified to write this most engaging overview to Mexico's pre-Columbian history. In a readable, easy-to-understand and unpretentious manner, he highlights the most important people, things and ideas of ancient Mexico. This is one of the best introductions to ancient Mexico written in English. The only unfortunate aspect about this noteworthy publication is that the black-and-white photographs do not convey the greatness of the cultures described. Notwithstanding this limitation, this is an extraordinary book.

Marnham, Patrick. So Far from God: A Journey to Central America. New York: Viking Press, 1985. 253 p. ISBN: 0-670-80449-5. $17.95. Gr. 9-adult.

Marnham's recent journey to California, Mexico, Costa
Rica, Guatemala, El Salvador, Honduras and Nicaragua is
recounted in an amusing and intelligent manner. His
mainly negative impressions are described honestly and
vividly. About Mexico: "The party which has governed
the country ever since has made corruption and the pursuit
of wealth its governmental emblem. The people are once
more at the mercy of greed and indifference" (p. 53).
Regarding his experiences at the Guatemalan consulate
in Mexico City, he states: "I remembered, but did not
mention, the old axiom that in Latin America officials
expect to be bribed to do their jobs. They do not expect to be bribed to break the law and if this is suggested
to them, they become upset" (p. 95). And, "In Guatemala
City, in 1984, it was said that for fifty American dollars,
you could hire an assassin who would ask no questions.
The price had not changed for two years, a tribute to
the stability of the currency" (p. 126). As a witty,
superficial view of Mexico and Central America, this book
offers light entertainment. It must be noted, however,
that this book has serious factual errors regarding
Mexican history, Guatemala's politics, Salvadoran leaders
and an incredibly faulty Spanish that is displayed throughout the whole book. His perceptions are wisely summarized
by the author: "The struggle between the United States
and New Spain seems to me to be a historical quarrel
rather than a political one. The people of North America
have little idea of religion, but they have a strict public
morality. The Latin people are without morality, but they
are highly religious. The two sides are attracted toward
each other, but they also feel mutual contempt" (p. 252).

Marrin, Albert. Aztecs and Spaniards: Cortés and the
Conquest of Mexico. New York: Atheneum, 1986. 212 p.
ISBN: 0-689-31176-1. $15.95. Gr. 7-10.

As a dynamic, engrossing account of the life of the Aztecs
in the XIV and XV centuries and of Cortés intrepid conquest of Mexico in 1519, this narrative is hard to surpass.
It is unfortunate, however, that the author chose to
dwell in over nine pages on the Aztec practice of human
sacrifice in all its gory detail as well as other "grisly
Aztec ceremonies" and barely mentioned in a few sentences
some of their positive achievements. In addition, some

historians may question the author's adulation of Cortés triumphs. Perhaps, if this were historical fiction, one would be more willing to forgive the author for his sloppy spelling of important Aztec and Spanish figures. The following words are misspelled throughout the book: "quetzel" [sic], "Quetzelcoatl" [sic] and "Navarez" [sic]. The poorly drawn black-and-white illustrations and photographs detract from the beauty of the original codexes and sculptures. As history, this book leaves much to be desired.

Martin, Patricia Preciado. Images and Conversations: Mexican Americans Recall a Southwestern Past. Photos by Louis Carlos Bernal. Tucson: University of Arizona Press, 1983. 110 p. ISBN: 0-8165-0801-1. $12.50. Gr. 9-adult.

Briefly, thirteen senior members of the Hispanic community of Arizona reminisce about their early lives. They narrate fond memories as well as abuses which they suffered by Anglo businessmen or the U.S. government. Sensitive black-and-white photographs of the speakers and places they recall add variety to the narratives.

*McKissack, Patricia. Aztec Indians. ISBN: 0-516-01936-8; The Inca. ISBN: 0-516-01268-1; The Maya. ISBN: 0-516-01270-3. Ea. Vol.: 48 p. (A New True Book) Chicago: Children's Press, 1985. $7.95. Gr. 2-4.

Easy-to-read texts and excellent photographs and illustrations in color provide young readers with an overview of these three outstanding pre-Columbian civilizations including their history, religion, language, customs and final days. Compared to many other books in English for young children about the Aztecs, Aztec Indians should be singled out for not emphasizing the Aztec practice of human sacrifice and for including important Aztec achievements. Reproductions of murals by the great Mexican artist, Diego Rivera, add immensely to the narrative. Inexplicably, there are two photographs from the Teotihuacan culture in Aztec Indians. There are only a few unfortunate statements in The Maya which mar this otherwise fine publication: The Mayan civilization is referred to as Central American—disregarding the fact that Mexico is part of North America. And, the following statements are unnecessary as they could apply to any culture in the world: "Quarrels resulted when the Maya drank too much honey wine. Family feuds were common" (p. 29). The Inca is definitely the best of the three books. The author provides much information in this dynamic, well-organized book with an outstanding selection of photographs and drawings.

McMeekin, Dorothy. Diego Rivera: Science and Creativity in the Detroit Murals./Ciencia y creatividad en los murales de Detroit. Spanish translation by María E.K. Moon. East Lansing: Michigan State University Press, 1985. 71 p. ISBN: 0-87013-239-3. $9.95. Gr. 9-adult.

The author definitely achieved her purpose in writing this book: to describe and explain the science in the twenty-seven murals in the Detroit Institute of Arts and to present a neglected part of Rivera's background—his knowledge of science. Admirers of the great Mexican muralist will be fascinated by Rivera's realism and by his symbols and analogies of the world of science. Interspersed in the text are mostly black-and-white and a few color photographs of the murals. One truly regrettable aspect of this publication is the awkward Spanish translation which is full of spelling, typographical and grammatical mistakes. There is no excuse for publishing such an inferior Spanish translation of the English text.

Meador, Nancy, and Betty Harman. Paco and the Lion of the North. Austin, Texas: Eakin Press, 1987. 117 p. ISBN: 0-89015-598-4. $8.95. Gr. 5-7.

Paco, a fourteen-year-old boy from a wealthy Mexican family, is abducted by Pancho Villa and his "bandidos." Fortunately, he is allowed to keep his beloved horse, Estrella, who accompanies him everywhere and protects him at difficult times. Northern Mexico and the Mexican Revolution provide an exciting setting for those readers interested in this turbulent era of Mexican history; others will be confused by the violence and cruelty and by the Mexican General, Pancho Villa, who "was the terror of the Río Grande Valley. He ranged freely on both sides of the river, killing, robbing, and looting for the supplies he needed to support his band of revolutionaries against the Mexican president, Venustiano Carranza, and the corrupt Mexican government" (p. v). Paco is a sympathetic character who manages to survive his captivity despite overwhelming odds, but the other characters are unconvincing and stale. This is historical fiction that tries hard to be fair to "both sides of the Rio Grande."

Mexico in Pictures. (Visual Geography Series) Minneapolis: Lerner Publications Company, 1987. 64 p. ISBN: 0-8225-1801-5. $9.95. Gr. 4-9.

Like other titles in this series, this book provides an overview of the land, history, government, people and economy of Mexico. It includes numerous photographs in color and black-and-white as well as a few well-selected maps. It is a readable, up-to-date introduction to Mexico. It is unfortunate, however, that even though it stresses the fact that most of the people in Mexico now live in urban areas, there are very few photographs which depict life in modern Mexico City. (Although it does include a photograph of a woman beggar at the side door of the Cathedral in Mexico City.) The majority of the photographs show a tourist's view of Mexico and its people--Indian markets, colorful crafts, tourist attractions and the ever-present rural scenes.

Meyer, Carolyn, and Charles Gallenkamp. The Mystery of the Ancient Maya. New York: Atheneum, 1985. 159 p. ISBN: 0-689-50319-9. $11.95. Gr. 7-12.

Maya achievements in art, architecture, mathematics, astronomy and writing are interestingly depicted in this simply written book with numerous black-and-white drawings and photographs. In vivid prose, the authors relate the excitement of the early explorers, the magnificence of the Classic Mayas, their sacrifices, their outstanding intellectual achievements, their everyday lives and their puzzling disappearance. It is unfortunate that none of the illustrations are in color, which would have conveyed much more dramatically the beauty of the original works. Despite this limitation, this is indeed a

most readable and informative introduction to the ancient
Maya civilization.

Miller, Mary Ellen. The Murals of Bonampak. Princeton:
Princeton University Press, 1986. 176 p. ISBN: 0-691-
04033-8. $67.50. Gr. 10-adult.

Despite the fact that the murals of Bonampak, Chiapas,
are hailed as the finest Classic Maya wall paintings, they
have received limited attention. Art lovers and serious
students of Mayan culture will be enthralled with this
spectacular volume with sixty-five beautiful color and
black-and-white reproductions of the murals. The scholarly
text may overwhelm some readers, but the author's thought-
ful explanations provide the reader with fresh insights
and new interpretations of what is now known about the
Classic Maya.

*Miller, Robert Ryal. Mexico: A History. Norman: Uni-
versity of Oklahoma Press, 1985. 414 p. ISBN: 0-8061-
1932-2. $19.95. Gr. 10-adult.

The principal characters, events and trends of Mexico's
exciting history are narrated by a knowledgeable professor of Mexican history. The narrative begins with a
description of early Indian cultures, followed by the
Spanish conquest, colonial institutions, the independence,
up to the modern era. Interspersed in the text are
numerous black-and-white photos as well as excerpts
from contemporary letters, books, decrees or poems that
add interest to each chapter. The first half of the book
is an unexciting recount of Mexico's early history in
strictly chronological order. Beginning with Chapter 7,
though, the narrative acquires a most stimulating momentum:
From the empire and early republic up to the modern era,
the author presents a well-balanced and informed perspective of the many problems, issues and dilemmas that have
tormented Mexico's development.

*Morley, Sylvanus G. and George W. Brainerd. The Ancient
Maya. 4th Rev. ed., Stanford, CA: Stanford University
Press, 1983. 708 p. ISBN: 0-8047-1137-2. $14.95.
Gr. 11-adult.

Serious students of the ancient Maya will be most interested in this revised edition prepared by Robert J. Sharer,
which preserves much of the original and highly esteemed
Morley-Brainerd text while at the same time incorporating
new discoveries and recent interpretations. Numerous
black-and-white photos, charts and maps and detailed text
describe the cultural history--setting, origins, preclassic,
classic and postclassic Maya; society--subsistence systems,
everyday life, trade and external conflict; material cul-
ture--architecture and archeaological sites, ceramics,
arts and crafts; and intellectual culture--ideology, language and writing, arithmetic, calendrics, and astronomy;
and the Spanish Conquest. This revised edition is essen-
tial reading for any student or would-be Mayan scholar.

Nicholson, Irene. Mexican and Central American Mythology.
[Rev. ed.] (Library of the World's Myths and Legends)
New York: Peter Bedrick Books, 1985. 144 p. ISBN:
0-87226-003-8. $17.95. Gr. 9-adult.

The myths of pre-Columbian Mexico are beautifully introduced to the general reader in what is supposed to be a
revised edition of the original version published in 1967.
Even though there is very little updating from the early
version, the outstanding color and black-and-white
photographs of pre-Columbian art and the informative
text make this an enticing introduction to the religion,
lore and legends of the Mayas, Aztecs, Mixtecs, Teoti-
huacans and other pre-Columbian people.

*¡Orozco! 1883-1949. edited by David Elliot. New York:
Universe Books, 1983. 128 p. ISBN: 0-87663-590-7.
pap. $9.95. Gr. 9-adult.

This is an excellent tribute to José Clemente Orozco, one
of Mexico's greatest muralists. It combines a photographic
record of his murals with various art critics' and specialists' comments on difference phases of his work. The
text is interspersed with numerous drawings, black-and-
white photographs, and unfortunately, a few color prints.
Even though the original impression is of an overcrowded
design, the book does a beautiful job of placing Orozco's
work in the context of social and political developments
in Mexico and the world.

*Pasztory, Esther. Aztec Art. New York: Harry N. Abrams, Inc., 1983. 335 p. ISBN: 0-8109-0687-2. $60.00. Gr. 9-adult.

The greatness of the Aztec empire has been beautifully preserved in this informative and heavily illustrated book. It includes chapters on the history and definition of Aztec art followed by chapters on Aztec architecture, major monuments, codices, stone sculptures, lapidary arts, wood sculpture and turquoise mosaic, featherwork, terracotta sculpture and ceramics. Even though most young adults do not have the background to understand the author's aesthetic analysis of Aztec art presented in this book, they will be impressed, nonetheless, by the dignity of the people who produced such beauty. The exquisite color and black-and-white photographs of Aztec art should entice neophytes to further explore the world of the Aztecs.

*Poniatowska, Elena. Dear Diego. Translated from Spanish by Katherine Silver. New York: Pantheon Books, 1986. 90 p. ISBN: 0-394-55383-7. $10.95. Gr. 9-adult.

Based on letters that Angelina Beloff wrote to the great Mexican artist, Diego Rivera, Poniatowska wrote this sad novel that describes Angelina's feeling of dejection upon the death of her infant son, the rejection and abandonment of her ten-year companion and her own struggles as an artist. Admirers of Diego Rivera will be moved by this brief novel that depicts the pain of unrequited love and a few glimpses of Diego's life in Paris in the 1910's.

Pronzini, Bill, and Martin H. Greenberg, eds. The Ethnic Detectives. New York: Dodd, Mead & Company, 1985. 360 p. ISBN: 0-396-08545-8. $16.95. Gr. 9-adult.

According to the editors, "an ethnic detective allows for the introductions of exotic characters, interesting cultural backgrounds, and sometimes unusual crimes" (p. x). Thus, in this anthology of seventeen mystery stories, the sleuth is "a member of a minority group within a dominant culture, one whose mannerisms, world view, and approach reflect his or her ethnic origins" (p. x). It includes oriental,

European, Jewish, native American and Hispanic detectives.
Some of the mysteries are authentic thrillers; others
abound in stereotypes such as the Mexican detective,
Vincente Lopez, in "The Hair of the Widow" by Robert
Somerlott, where all Mexico is a ridiculous caricature.
Much more authentic is the Chicana detective, Elena
Oliverez in "the Sanchez Sacraments" by Marcia Muller.

Purdy, Susan, and Cass R. Sandak. Aztecs. Illustrated
by Pamela Ford Johnson. (A Civilization Project Book)
New York: Franklin Watts, 1982. 32p. ISBN: 0-531-
04455-6. $4.95. Gr. 5-7.

Ostensibly, this book provides a background to Aztec
civilization and a guide for creating replicas of Aztec cultural artifacts, such as masks, shields, cloaks, carvings,
drums, jugs, helmets and foods. The information about
Aztec civilization is so scanty and poorly written that it
makes this book inadequate as introductory reading. And,
the black-and-white illustrations and diagrams reduce
Aztec civilization to a quick-and-dirty curio workshop.
Young readers will not be impressed with Aztec civilization through the "projects" or information provided in
this book.

*Rediscovered Masterpieces of Mesoamerica: Mexico--Guatemala--
Honduras. Edited by Gérald Berjonneau and Jean-Louis
Sonnery. New York: Rizzoli, 1986. 288 p. ISBN:
0-8478-0709-6. $75.00. Gr. 10-adult.

Lovers of pre-Columbian art will relish in this outstanding
book which includes dramatic photographs in color and
black-and-white from secret collections of unknown masterpieces. Unpublished art works from pre-Columbian Mexico
and Central America which could only be seen in private
collections and museum storerooms can now be admired in
this well designed and lavishly illustrated first volume of
the forthcoming series, "Rediscovered Masterpieces."
East chapter--The Gulf Coast, Central Mexico and Oaxaca,
The Pacific Coast, and The Maya--includes a readable
introduction which adds to the understanding of the
various cultures discussed. This is definitely for sophisticated art lovers.

Ribaroff, Margaret Flesher. Mexico and the United States
Today: Issues Between Neighbors. New York: Franklin
Watts, Inc., 1985. 104 p. ISBN: 0-531-04757-1. $10.90.
Gr. 8-12.

The three major issues between the U.S. and Mexico today--
maintaining a profitable trading partnership, resolving the
dilemma of undocumented workers in the United States,
and reconciling deep-seated differences over political
change in Central America--are exmined in this carefully
researched book. Difficult issues are explained both from
a historical and a bilateral political perspective, making
this book a good source of information about complex contemporary political and economic differences between the
U.S. and Mexico. A good selection of black-and-white
photographs and a well-written text certainly add to the
readers' understanding of these issues. There is only
one aspect about this book that must be criticized: The
author is very open and direct in blaming United States'
policies towards Mexico in several instances; yet, she is
much more subtle and guarded in her discussion of Mexico's
policies or internal problems. This lack of balance in dis-
cussing the two countries detracts from what could have
been a truly objective analysis of the difficult problems
between Mexico and the U.S. today.

*Riding, Alan. Distant Neighbors: Portrait of the Mexicans.
New York: Alfred A. Knopf, 1985. 385 p. ISBN: 0-
394-50005-9. $18.45. Gr. 10-adult.

This is a most comprehensive analysis of Mexico and its
people written by a longtime New York times correspondent
based in Mexico City until 1984. As a good journalist,
Mr. Riding reports on contemporary events with much
candor and, in most cases, great objectivity. This ambi-
tious book includes discussions on Mexico's history, political system, agriculture, petroleum industry, cultural life,
social problems, foreign policy as well as chapters on corruption, Mexico-U.S. relations and an uncertain future.
And this, perhaps, may be an obstacle for some readers
who will have to overcome a thousand facts, names and
government projects, many times repeatedly, to understand
Mr. Riding's perceptions of Mexico's chronic inefficiency,
corruption, mismanagement, poverty and injustice. Despite

the excellence of this journalistic feat, one wonders why
Mr. Riding cautions Mexicans against giving in to the
demands of the middle-class, which he calls, the "Ameri-
canized minority," and pretentiously recommends the system
turn inward to a mixture of "authoritarianism and pater-
nalism, of cynicism and idealism, of conciliation of nego-
tiation" (p. 371). There are a few unfortunate, ethno-
centric conclusions in what is otherwise a most well-informed
book on Mexico and its people.

Santiago, Danny. <u>Famous All Over Town</u>. New York: Simon
& Schuster, Inc., 1983. 185 p. ISBN: 0-671-43249-4.
$14.95. Gr. 9-adult.

Rudy Medina, Jr., better known as Chato, is a most
perceptive young man, who narrates in a dynamic and
engrossing manner, the events that dominated his life
during his last year in his Mexican-American neighborhood
of eastside Los Angeles: His mother has a baby at home,
his best friend is killed by the police, he and his family
take a depressing trip to Mexico which is full of the cus-
tomary poverty and Mexican abuses, his father's constant
drinking and womanizing, the marriage of his older sister,
and, finally, the dissolution of his family. As an emotion-
packed story with engaging characters, this story will be
read by great interest by many young adults. It is unfortunate, however, that so many readers will be reinforced
in their stereotypes about Mexico and its people by the
so-called "authenticity" of this story. There is no doubt
that the author, regardless of his nationality, has produced
a most engrossing story. What is most disturbing to me
is the almost obsessive view that the author projects of
Mexican people, either in Los Angeles or in a small town
in Mexico: Mexican man, who always drink in excess and
abuse women; Mexican women who lack courage and "accept
their place in society," and the lack of any beauty and
joy in Mexico. This novel, as a description of the life of
one Mexican-American family, is definitely authentic; yet,
one does not want to read exclusively about poor, unedu-
cated Mexicans and "dirty old Mexico."

Somonte, Carlos. <u>We Live in Mexico</u>. (Living Here Series)
New York: The Bookwright Press, 1985. 60 p. ISBN:

01-531-03820-3. $9.90. Gr. 4-8. Distributed by:
Franklin Watts, Inc.

Like other titles in this series, this book includes first-
person interviews with twenty-six different Mexicans de-
scribing their lives and occupations as well as the area of
the country in which they live. Striking, colorful photographs complement the informative two-page interviews.
It is unfortunate, however, that, with a few exceptions,
most of the people interviewed are either blue collar or
rural workers reinforcing the common stereotype of poor
Mexicans in quaint rural settings anxious to trade with
American tourists.

*Stein, R. Conrad. Mexico. Chicago: Children's Press, 1984.
126 p. (Enchantment of the World). ISBN: 0-516-02772-7.
$10.95. Gr. 4-8.

The amazing variety and contrasts of Mexico's geography,
history, economy, culture, government and people are
interestingly described in this well-written introduction
to our neighbor to the south. Attractive color photographs
capture the beauty and joy of Mexico. In addition, the
author needs to be commended for explaining in an honest
and straightforward manner the problems of Mexico today,
such as Mexico's severe unemployment, poverty, and smog
in Mexico City. The only regrettable note, in this otherwise oustanding introductory book, is the large number of
misaccented, misspelled or misused words in Spanish.

*Tuck, Jim. Pancho Villa and John Reed: Two Faces of
Romantic Revolution. Tucson: University of Arizona
Press, 1984. 252 p. ISBN: 0-8165-0867-4. $16.95.
Gr. 10-adult.

The passion, idealism and high sense of adventure with
which Pancho Villa and John Reed approach revolution are
described in this engrossing narrative. Written as a
parallel biography about "these supremely appealing and
charismatic figures," it examines their lives, their brief
encounter in revolutionary Mexico, and their successes and
ultimate defeats. Pancho Villa's Mexico and John Reed's
communist activities in the U.S. and the Soviet Union are

described with candor and objectivity. Young adults
will be fascinated by these "romantic revolutionaries" who,
according to the author, belong to the "'hard' romantic
faction: romantic without being sentimental and idealistic
without being mushy" (p. 208).

Verheyden-Hilliard, Mary Ellen. Scientist with Determination,
Elma González. Illustrated by Marian Menzel. (American
Women in Science Biography) Bethesda, MD: Equity
Institute, 1985. 31 p. ISBN: 0-932469-01-9. $3.95.
Gr. 3-5.

Despite the unassuming presentation of this paperback
book with simple black-and-white drawings, young readers
will be inspired by this scientist with determination who
is born in Mexico, works with her family as a migrant
farm worker, starts school when she is nine years old and,
finally, goes to college to earn her doctorate in cellular
biology. This easy-to-read biography is a positive and
optimistic depiction of a likeable and successful Mexican-
American female scientist.

Weinberger, Eliot, ed. Octavio Paz: Selected Poems. New
York: New Directions Publishing Corporation, 1985. 147
p. ISBN: 0-8112-0903-2. $10.50. Gr. 11-adult.

Octavio Paz, one of Latin America's best-known poets, was
born in Mexico in 1914. This edition includes 67 of his
poems translated into English by eleven prominent authors
and poets. As a great surrealist poet, Paz's poetry will
appeal to young adults who have the necessary background
and sophistication to understand and admire a Mexican poet
who depicts the workings of the unconscious mind. Several
of his phases and styles are represented in this selection.

*Weisman, Alan. La Frontera: The United States Border
with Mexico. Photographs by Jay Dusard. San Diego:
Harcourt Brace Jovanovich, 1986. 200 p. ISBN: 0-15-
147315-3. $19.95. Gr. 9-adult.

The people, cities and countryside along the two-thousand-
mile border between Mexico and the United States are

described in an incisive narrative and 56 outstanding, black-and-white photographic plates. With a great deal of honesty and understanding, the author tells about the serious issues surrounding both Mexican and American people in the region such as poverty, unemployment, prostitution, corruption, drug smuggling, illegal immigration and others. Extensive, poignant interviews of the people who live in the area and sensitive photographs result in a moving social documentary of this bilingual, bicultural society.

*Wepman, Dennis. Benito Juárez. (World Leaders Past & Present) New York: Chelsea House Publishers, 1986. 115 p. ISBN: 0-87754-537-5. $15.95. Gr. 8-12.

Benito Juárez was a Zapotec Indian and one of Mexico's most extraordinary political figures and presidents. This highly objective and most readable biography provides an insightful view of Mexico in the nineteenth century and of the public life of this great man. "Born into a country with an oppressively traditional class system, [Juárez] transformed himself from an illiterate shepherd boy into the nation's most powerful magistrate. In an era hugely complicated by military dictators, civil wars, banditry, and foreign intervention, he distinguished himself as a civilian who unfailingly placed his country's welfare above his own" (p. 110). Any reader who wishes to understand Mexico of the nineteenth century and the life of one of its most dedicated men will be enthralled with this biography. Numerous black-and-white reproductions of prints, photographs, and paintings add to the value of this historical narrative.

NICARAGUA

Adams, Faith. Nicaragua: Struggling with Change. (Dis-
covering our Heritage) Minneapolis: Dillon Press, Inc.,
1987. 149 p. ISBN: 0-87518-340-5. $12.95. Gr. 5-8.

Ostensibly, the purpose of this book is to introduce readers
to the geography, culture, history and politics of Nicaragua. But its overriding goals are to praise the Sandinistas by emphasizing their numerous accomplishments and
to blame the Contras for all the problems of Nicaragua
today. And, of course, the United States government
and the Reagan administration are especially guilty:
"Nicaraguans consider baseball to be one of the good
things they received from the United States: (p. 120).
Numerous color photographs accompany the politically
biased text.

Cabestrero, Teófilo. Blood of the Innocent: Victims of the
Contras' War in Nicaragua. Translated by Robert R. Barr.
New York: Orbis Books, 1985. 104 p. ISBN: 0-88344-
211-6. $6.95. Gr. 9-adult.

Cabestrero, a Catholic priest, reports on the testimony
of some sixty persons who were "the victims of kidnappings,
bloody ambushes, rapes and other assaults by the contras."
It is obvious that the author's intent is to blame President
Reagan's policies for the abuses, murders, and destruction committed by the Contras in Nicaragua. Through the
voices of innocent victims, the reader is exposed to a
constant barrage of suffering and death and to accusations
against current U.S. policies in Nicaragua.

Cabezas, Omar. Fire from the Mountain: The making of a Sandinista. Translated by: Kathleen Weaver. New York: Crown Publishers, 1985. 233 p. ISBN: 0-517-55800-9. $13.95. Gr. 9-adult.

Omar Cabezas, a commandante in the Nicaraguan armed forces and Chief of Political Direction at the Ministry of the Interior in the Sandinista government, relates his early experiences as a guerrilla in the movement that overthrew Somoza. In a touching, human, amusing, yet confusing and redundant manner he tells about his fears, doubts, loneliness and adventures in the mountains of Nicaragua. Admirers of the Sandinistas will enjoy this earthy memoir of a successful revolutionary; others will be confused by the lack of dates and basic background information; and others might be offended by the explicit language and references to prostitution and sexual experiences.

Cardenal, Ernesto. With Walker in Nicaragua and other early poems, 1949-1954. Selected and translated by Jonathan Cohen. Middletown, CT: Wesleyan University Press, 1984. 111 p. ISBN: 0-8195-5123-6. $17.00. Gr. 10-adult.

This bilingual collection of poems by the activist poet and Nicaraguan Minister of Culture since 1979, Ernesto Cardenal, recounts in a colorful and robust manner the history and people of his native Nicaragua. It also includes an informative introduction by the translator, Jonathan Cohen, which discusses the development of Cardenal's poetry as an emerging realist, "the work of a poet committed to social justice and human dignity" (p. 3), as well as Cardenal's mastery of understatement and sense of humor "which often saves his poetry from falling into rhetorial bombast" (p. 12).

*Christian, Shirley. Nicaragua: Revolution in the Family. New York: Random House, 1985. 337 p. ISBN: 0-394-53575-8. $19.95. Gr. 10-adult.

Christian, a Pulitzer-Prize Winner in International Reporting, has written a detailed reconstruction of events before and

after the Sandinistas' coming to power in Nicaragua.
Through years of interviews, on-the-scene observations
and discerning use of news accounts, she has produced
a timely, informative and objective report of this controversial area of Central America. There is no question
that many readers--from the extreme left or the extreme
right--will find fault with some of the issues presented by
Ms. Christian, but despite her own personal beliefs, one
must give her credit for examining and reporting in an
even-handed manner the dynamics of Nicaragua's present
political turmoil. Readers who are interested in a brief
discussion of the current dilemmas facing the United
States in Nicaragua will find the epilogue (pp. 305-311)
particularly explicit and candid.

Dickey, Christopher. With the Contras: A Reporter in the
    Wilds of Nicaragua. New York: Simon & Schuster, 1985.
    327 p. ISBN: 0-671-53298-7. $18.95. Gr. 9-adult.

Christopher Dickey, a Washington Post Correspondent, provides a detailed narrative about the people, issues and
politics involved in Nicaragua's brutal war since 1979,
the year the dictator Anastasio Somoza left Nicaragua. In
a personal and touching manner, he recounts his experiences
as an American journalist in the mountains of Nicaragua
with the Contras as well as his perceptions of the inscru-
table war that is being waged against the Sandinista government and funded by the United States. The author's
strongest criticism is reserved for the CIA and the Reagan
Administration. He concludes: "The fight continued, now,
with no end in sight and the constant threat that the
Reagan administration, having committed itself to the
Sandinistas' overthrow, would finally decide it had no
option but open, direct U.S. military action if the Contras
falter once too often or too badly. The army was still in
the field. The war was not over" (p. 271).

Dixon, Marlene, ed. On Trial: Reagan's War Against Nicara-
    gua. San Francisco: Synthesis Publications, 1985. 269 p.
    ISBN: 0-89935-042-9. $9.95. Gr. 10-adult.

This report of the Permanent Peoples' Tribunal is a one-
sided indictment against the U.S. and specifically the

Reagan administration for its policies in Nicaragua. Nicaraguan government officials, selected civilians and the editor of this publication, who is Director of the Institute for the study of Militarism and Economic Crisis in San Francisco and editor of its journal, Contemporary Marxism, incessantly reiterate the belief that: "Throughout its history, Nicaragua has experienced political, economic and military attack and intervention by North American imperialism" (p. 1). And, "other charges against the government of Ronald Reagan are: mercenarian, manipulation of regional organizations, and complicity with genocidal regimes" (p. 26). For those eager to read and see black-and-white pictures that provide "evidence" of the brutality of U.S. policies, this "trial" will satisfy them; others should search for a less passionate and more objective view of Reagan's politices in Nicaragua.

Eich, Dieter, and Carlos Rincón. The Contras: Interviews with Anti-Sandinistas. Translated by Margot Brunner and others. San Francisco: Synthesis Publications, 1985. 193 p. ISBN: 0-89935-051-8. $7.95. Gr. 10-adult.

For those interested in reading a barrage of anti-American propaganda, these interviews provide "evidence" about the counter-revolutionaries who seek to overthrow the Sandinistas. These selected interviews monotonously reiterate the feelings and beliefs of mostly men who wish to destabilize "the revolutionary government." It appears that the main purpose of this book is to provide evidence that, by backing the Contras, the United States supports terrorist actions. One of the interviewees explains: "Arafat is supported by Libya, there is no doubt about this, and we are supported in the same way by the United States. Every revolution is supported by a foreign power" (p. 39). Dull interviews with an obvious political message.

Everett, Melissa. Bearing Witness, Building Bridges: Interviews with North Americans Living & Working in Nicaragua. Philadelphia: New Society Publishers, 1986. 169 p. ISBN: 0-86571-065-1. $8.95. Gr. 9-adult.

Seventeen Americans who have chosen to "let go of the relative safety and comfort of life in the United States in

order to live in a much more challenging environment:
Postrevolutionary Nicaragua" are interviewed here. According to the introduction, they "are all supportive of
the stated goals of that revolution: redistribution of resources in favor of the poor; political pluralism; a mixed
economy with a strong public sector; and nonalignment in
foreign relations" (xvi). Many of the interviewees are
religious workers and most of them are enthusiastic supporters of the Sandinistas in Nicaragua. They report on
the outstanding achievements made by the Sandinistas and
blame the Reagan administration's support of the Contras:
"Life can be hard down here sometimes for someone from
the States. Particularly with Reagan's economic and military war, there are lots of shortages, and none of the
amenities we're used to" (p. 59). I can't imagine young
adults being interested in these long, passionate testimonials
about the wonders of the Sandinistas.

Grossman, Karl. Nicaragua: America's New Vietnam? Sag
   Harbor, NY: Permanent Press, 1985. 228 p. ISBN:
   0-932966-46-2. $10.95. Gr. 10-adult.

The author, an investigative reporter, records his journey,
investigation, impressions and discoveries to warn the
reader to what "some say could be a new Vietnam." Thus,
from the moment he arrives in Honduras, he starts condemn-
ing U.S. influences in Central America. Later, he reports
on his visit to the war zone of Nicaragua, his talks with
supporters of the Sandinista revolution, and his talks with
opponents of the Sandinista government who "suggest [that]
the Sandinista revolution has faults" (p. 87). Through
interviews of a few individuals, he reports on religion,
politics and Americans in Nicaragua. His inevitable conclusion: "What the United States is up to in Nicaragua is
illegal, immoral and impractical. And if it escalates--
and the Reagan administration seems to have a compulsive
desire to have it escalate--a Vietnam-style war is what
would be ahead" (p. 195). This is one person's opinion
of the many issues between the U.S. and Nicaragua. It is
not, however, an insightful or discerning analysis of the
many issues between Nicaragua and the U.S. today.

Hanmer, Trudy J. Nicaragua. New York: Franklin Watts,
   1986. 66 p. ISBN: 0-531-10125-8. $9.40. Gr. 5-8.

In a bland monotone, the author attempts to answer two
questions about Nicaragua. How has Nicaragua become
the site of so much turmoil? And, how did Nicaragua
become the culturally mixed, politically turbulent nation
that it is today? By including chapters on the land, the
history, the people and the customs of Nicaragua, the
reader is supposed to be able to answer these questions.
I doubt that most readers will. As an unexciting overview to Nicaragua, this narrative may assist some readers.

*Haverstock, Nathan. Nicaragua in Pictures. (Visual Geo-
graphy Series). Minneapolis: Lerner Publications, 1987.
64 p. ISBN: 0-8225-1817-1. $9.95. Gr. 6-12.

Like Haverstock's Cuba in Pictures, this is a most objective and concise introduction to the land, history, government, people and economy of Nicaragua. Numerous black-
and-white and color photographs and the author's direct
narrative explain the successes--"The Sandinista government has scored a success in its national campaign to
promote literacy" (p. 46)--and limitations--"The government
has imposed controls and censorships on all information
media, which are expected to support the goals of the
revolution" (p. 48). Readers interested in understanding
many of the complex issues surrounding this Central American country, including U.S. economic and military pres-
sures, will not be disappointed in this new edition.

Levie, Alvin. Nicaragua: The People Speak. South Hadley,
MA: Bergin & Garvey Publishers, Inc., 1985. 198 p.
ISBN: 0-89789-083-3. $24.95. Gr. 9-adult.

Brief interviews of the common people of Nicaragua con-
ducted by the author, Witness for Peace activist, Alan
Levie, are the basis of this anti-American view of contemporary Nicaragua. In the preface, the author recounts
the successes of Nicaragua's revolution and states that
"Unquestionably, my sympathies are not neutral. But in
telling the story of the people of Nicaragua I have tried
to be an honest reporter..." (p. xxiii). Even though a
few of the interviews reflect a lack of enthusiasm for
Nicaragua's revolutionary government, most of the interviews tell of the great improvements made by the revolution.

And, predictably, many criticize Reagan and U.S. policies, such as: "But as long as we suffer the aggression, things won't improve. First of all, there's economic aggression from the United States. Then there's the military aggression" (p. 86). It is obvious that in his brief trip to Nicaragua Mr. Levie heard and saw what he originally wanted to report.

Nicaragua Under Siege. Edited by Marlene Dixon and Susan Jonas. (Contemporary Marxism) San Francisco: Synthesis Publications, 1984. 234 p. ISBN: 0-89935-036-4. $8.95. Gr. 10-adult.

This is a violent, leftist impassioned condemnation of the Reagan Administration and of U.S. foreign policy in Central America. The editors gathered interviews, Nicaraguan government documents and articles that "convey to an American public that time and time again has expressed its opposition to U.S. intervention in Central America, the realities of U.S. aggression, as well as the vitality and originality of the Nicaraguan Revolution" (xv). Incessantly, the authors accuse the U.S. government: "Reagan acts only because he exploits the near-monarchical powers which are invested in a President of the United States, urged on by hard-line right-wingers such as former National Security Adviser William Clark, and completely unhampered by a gutless U.S. Congress" (p. 13) and praise the current Nicaraguan government: "...what has really impressed me is the love for democracy in Nicaragua and there is much more democracy than we have in the United States" (p. 197). The obvious heroes in this political manifesto are the representatives of the Sandinista People's Revolution and the genuine villains are the representatives of U.S. "imperialism and capitalism."

Ridenour, Ron. Yankee Sandinistas: Interviews with North Americans Living & Working in the new Nicaragua. Willimantic, CT: Curbstone Press, 1986. 175 p. ISBN: 0-915306-62-X. $17.50. Gr. 9-adult.

The author, who describes himself as "an angry American citizen," interviewed nine people from the United States "who live and work in Nicaragua, helping to create 'el nuevo hombre' (the new person). To do so, they must by definition fight against their government's persistent policies of controlling other nations" (p. 10). Hence, it is not surprising that these people "became emotionally disgusted with everything in the United States" (p. 49), and that so many believe that "Ending imperialism and transforming social conditions in the U.S. will give the working people a better shake than they have" (p. 130.) The interviews cover the subjects' current activities as well as a discussion of their backgrounds and their reasons for moving to Central America. This is one more book on Central America which criticizes Reagan's foreign policy.

Rosset, Peter, and John Vandermeer, eds. Nicaragua: Unfinished Revolution--The New Nicaragua Reader. New York: Grove Press, Inc., 1986. 505 p. $22.95. ISBN: 0-394-55242-3. Gr. 9-adult.

The obvious purpose of this collection of articles, policy statements, eyewitness reports, documents and opinions is to present a pro-Sandinista view of Nicaragua. Only readers interested in political rhetoric blaming the U.S. and praising the Sandinista government will be able to plow through this volume. Perhaps the only unexpected article in this collection is Robert Leiken's "Nicaragua's Untold Stories," reprinted from The New Republic, which presents a negative view of life in Nicaragua under the Sandinistas. Otherwise, most readers know what to expect from collections such as this one.

Rosset, Peter, and John Vandermeer, eds. The Nicaraguan Reader: Documents of a Revolution Under Fire. New York: Grove Press, Inc., 1983. 362 p. ISBN: 0-394-53506-5. $13.50. Gr. 11-adult.

Peter Rosset, a doctoral student in agriculture and John Vandermeer, a Professor of Ecology at the University of Michigan, have collected sixty-one essays, articles and excerpts by journalists, academics and special-interest groups in four areas: the debate between Nicaragua and the U.S., historical setting, U.S. intervention and life in the new Nicaragua. From the outset the editors state:

"we cannot claim to be impartial ... we feel that true impartiality on political questions does not exist ... we must ... confess our belief that as a sovereign country Nicaragua has a right to its own self-determination" (p. xv). Thus, in one way or another most of the authors of these selections ultimately blame the U.S.: "the people of Nicaragua have been suffering under the yoke of a reactionary clique imposed by Yankee imperialism.... This clique has reduced Nicaragua to the status of a neocolony, exploited by the Yankee monopolies and the local capitalist class" (p. 126), or, specifically, Ronald Reagan. This is dull, up-to-date, political propaganda.

Rushdie, Salman. The Jaguar Smile: A Nicaraguan Journey. New York: Viking Penguin, Inc., 1987. 171 p. ISBN: 0-670-81757. $12.95. Gr. 9-adult.

Rushdie, an Indian novelist, was invited to Nicaragua for three weeks in July, 1986, by the Sandinista Association of Cultural Workers. From the beginning, the author's anti-U.S. bias is evident. He sees ugly American symbols everywhere and he writes: "It was impossible to spend even a day in Nicaragua without becoming aware of the huge and unrelenting pressure being exerted on the country by the giant standing on its northern frontier. It was a pressure that informed every minute of every day" (p. 37). Even though the author disagrees with the Sandinistas on the issue of freedom of the press ("It disturbed me that a government of writers had turned into a government of censors" [p. 48]), this is basically an admiring portrait of Nicaragua under the Sandinistas. It is thus difficult to comprehend why most of the Spanish words in the narrative are misspelled: "dío" [sic], "culpabile" [sic], "Palácio" [sic], "miede" [sic].

Zwerling, Philip, and Connie Martin. Nicaragua: A New Kind of Revolution. Westport, CT: Lawrence Hill & Company, 1985. 251 p. ISBN: 0-88208-181-0. $18.95. Gr. 9-adult.

Philip Zwerling, a Unitarian minister, and his wife, Connie Martin, spent six months traveling and interviewing mainly top Sandinista officials and a few common people in Nicaragua. Not surprisingly, the results, with a few exceptions,

are a series of interviews that describe in glowing terms
the tremendous successes of the Sandinistas: "There are
so many areas to speak of: education, financial support
for poor people, medical care, government technical aid
to peasants, building projects of new homes, the promotion
of the dignity of women" (p. 23). Of course, it also includes the inevitable attacks to the Reagan administration
and the United States. Rosario Murillo, wife of President
Daniel Ortega, states: "The only fear I have is the effect
of the CIA and North American terror here in Nicaragua.
Our children ought to be able to live free of fear and
trauma" (p. 42). One more passionate report on the
Sandinistas in Nicaragua.

PANAMA

Panama in Pictures. (Visual Geography Series) Minneapolis:
  Lerner Publications Company, 1987. 64 p. ISBN: 0-
  8225-1818-X. $9.95. Gr. 5-10.

Panama is introduced to young readers in this updated
edition which includes chapters on the land, history,
government, the people and the economy. Young readers
will definitely notice a difference between the older black-
and-white photos and the newer full-color photographs.
Young readers will be especially interested on sections
which discuss the Panama Canal, both from a historical
and a contemporary perspective.

Panama Post Report. Washington, DC: Department of State,
  September 1984. 19 p. (S/N-044-000-02028-9) $4.95. Gr.
  7-12.

This official post report is prepared by the post for official
U.S. Government employees and their families. As such,
it includes basic information about the host country--
Panama--and information about the American Embassy as
well as temporary and permanent housing facilities for U.S.
post personnel. This is a basic overview to life in Panama's
diplomatic circle.

PERU

Cross, Gillian. Born of the Sun. New York: Holiday House, Inc., 1983. 229 p. ISBN: 0-8234-0528-1. $11.95. Gr. 8-10. (See annotation under "Bolivia")

*McKissack, Patricia. Aztec Indians; The Inca. (See review under "Mexico")

Morrison, Marion. Atahuallpa and the Incas. Illustrated by Gerry Wood. (Life and Times) New York: The Bookwright Press, 1986. 59 p. ISBN: 0-531-18080-8. $10.90. Gr. 4-8.

Through Atahuallpa, the last of the great Inca rulers, young readers are introduced to the Inca Empire, including Inca legends, social and political organization, daily life, and the conquest of the Incas by the Spaniards. The worst aspect of this book are the gaudy, crude illustrations which, at best, ridicule the Incas. The dry, unexciting text provides only a series of unrelated facts which do not do justice to the Inca civilization.

Peru in Pictures. (Visual Geography Series) Minneapolis: Lerner Publications Company, 1987. 64 p. ISBN: 0-8225-1820-1. $9.95. Gr. 5-10.

Peru's land, history, government, people and economy are described through a direct, easy-to-read text and numerous black-and-white and color photographs. The chapters on the history and the economy will be of special interest to young readers who need good summaries of these areas.

The new full-color photographs in this updated version are a definite improvement over the older black-and-white photos which have been retained.

*Ridgway, John. Road to Osambre: A Daring Adventure in the High Country of Peru. New York: Viking, 1986. 244 p. ISBN: 0-670-81650-7. $18.95. Gr. 9-adult.

The isolated mountains of Peru are the background for this exciting narrative which recounts the author's daring expedition with his wife, eighteen-year-old daughter and two young men. Amidst the poverty and terrorism of Peru in the 1980s, readers will experience the trials of a dangerous journey as well as the simple joys of friendship and the beauty of nature. This is, indeed a moving account of the suffering of many innocent people in the highlands of Peru.

St. John, Jetty. A Family in Peru. Photos by Nigel Harvey. Minneapolis: Lerner Publications Company, 1987. 31 p. ISBN: 0-8225-1669-1. $8.95. Gr. 3-6.

Excellent photographs in color and an easy-to-read text describe the home, customs, work, school, and amusements of a Peruvian girl and her family who live in a small town high in an Andean mountain. This is a pleasing introduction to the Incas in Peru.

PUERTO RICO

*LaBrucherie, Roger A. Images of Puerto Rico. El Centro,
 CA: Imágenes Press, distr. by Tuttle, 1985. [148 p.]
 ISBN: 0930302-01-1. $21.95. Gr. 7-adult.

Spectacular photographs in color are the basis of this
photographic essay on Puerto Rico, which includes chapters
on the history, heritage, "jíbaro," the island, "New" San
Juan, today in Puerto Rico, natural resources and Old
San Juan. The author does not pretend to offer an in-
depth analysis of Puerto Rican history, culture or society
but rather a verbal and visual collection of personal impressions and observations which he gathered during the
five months that he spent on the island. Hence, this book
reflects the author's subjective interpretations of Puerto
Rico's past, present and future. Unfortunately, it does
not contain a table of contents nor an index which may
limit its use for those desiring specific information on
Puerto Rico. Notwithstanding these limitations, this is a
gorgeous visual panorama of Puerto Rico. (This book is
also available in Spanish.)

*Mohr, Nicholasa. Going Home. New York: Dial books for
 Young Readers, 1986. 192 p. ISBN: 0-8037-0338-4.
 $11.89. Gr. 5-8.

Through Felita, a delightful eleven-year-old girl, readers
will empathize with the problems and joys of a Puerto
Rican girl. Felita's Puerto Rican family is definitely authentic including a normal family's squabbles and misunder-
standings. In addition, the problems of growing up in a
bilingual, bicultural society--in New York and in Puerto
Rico--are touchingly and sensitively portrayed. All

readers will sympathize with Felita's determination; Hispanic young readers will especially identify with Felita's
feelings of rejection through the actions of uncaring,
narrow-minded children. This is a most enjoyable story
with a strong Puerto Rican flavor.

Molina, María. Menudo. Translated by Elizabeth García.
Photos by Juan Ruiz. New York: Julian Messner, 1984.
96 p. ISBN: 0-671-50635-8. $8.79. Gr. 5-8.

Confirmed Menudo fans might be tempted to skim through
this bilingual (English/Spanish) book that gives basic
facts about the members of the group, their music, movies,
travels, merchandise and fans. Other readers will be
uninspired by what seem to be hastily put together pro-
motional brochures about these charming performers.
Some of the black-and-white photographs will definitely
appeal to young readers. The intermixing of the English
and Spanish texts, however, does not make for easy reading. And, Spanish readers will be annoyed by the awkward translation.

Morales Carrión, Arturo, ed. Puerto Rico: A Political and
Cultural History. New York: W. W. Norton and Com-
pany, 1983. 384 p. ISBN: 0-393-01740-0. $19.50.
Gr. 9-adult.

According to the authors, "A prime consideration of this
book is to establish a more balanced perspective of what
Puerto Rico constitutes as a people, a cultural nationality,
or a distinctive Caribbean entity ... to the attention of
the reader in the United States" (p. x). The first part
of the book discusses the pre-1898 period including the
Indian inheritance, the arrival of the Spanish type of
western civilization, and the Puerto Rican struggle for
self-determination. The second part deals with the
twentieth century, especially the "complex colonial or
dependent relationship with the United States" and a
most informative chapter on the evolution of Puerto Rico's
cultural traditions. Morales, the editor and author of
the second part of this book is especially concerned about
the U.S. and its attitude towards Puerto Rico: "In
Puerto Rico, the United States is subject to a difficult

test. It is a test of both its altruism and its national egoism; its capacity to understand and its proclivity to misunderstand, its mature world view and its self-centered parochialism" (p. 316).

Nelson, Anne. <u>Murder Under Two Flags: The U.S., Puerto Rico, and the Cerro Maravilla Cover-up</u>. New York: Ticknor & Fields, 1986. 269 p. ISBN: 0-89919-371-4. $17.45. Gr. 10-adult.

The author states in the introduction that "this is not a history book," yet more than half of this narrative discusses the history of Puerto Rico and explains why "Puerto Rico's halfway status is a sickness that has poisoned its political life" (p. 2). In addition, she states that "As long as the island's status is undefined, Puerto Rico is condemned to continue the cycle of violence that has been going on for decades" (p. 2). The second half of this book tells about two young men who were killed by Puerto Rican police in July 25, 1978, on top of a mountain called Cerro Maravilla. Differing from official accounts, Nelson argues that these two young men were idealistic "independistas" who became unwitting victims of Puerto Rico's pro-statehood government. This is a one-sided view of Puerto Rico political issues.

<u>Puerto Rico in Pictures</u>. (Visual Geography Series) Minneapolis: Lerner Publications Company, 1987. 64 p. ISBN: 0-8225-1821-X. $9.95. Gr. 4-8.

Puerto Rico is introduced to young readers in this basic guide. It includes chapters on the land, history, government, the people and the economy as well as numerous black-and-white and color photographs. Even though there is nothing particularly exciting about this new edition, it does include updated information on Puerto Rico.

Reilly, Pat. <u>Kidnap in San Juan</u>. New York: Dell Publishing Company, 1984. 91 p. ISBN: 0-440-94460-0. $2.25. Gr. 4-6.

Marie, a fifteen-year-old, and her sister Carol, who is only

five, decide to stay in Old San Juan while their parents
are sight-seeing elsewhere on the island. Suddenly, a
woman grabs Carol and drags her into a car. Thus begins
this quick-paced mystery that includes an innocent kidnapped girl, a false policeman, a fast trip to Colombia to
get cocaine for the kidnappers, and a brave heroine that
ultimately saves her sister and fools the kidnappers and
drug dealers. Unfortunately, San Juan (Puerto Rico) and
Bogotá (Colombia) are depicted as the scenes of crime and
drugs, with no mention of anything else. But this is
definitely an attention grabber with lots of action and many
black-and-white photographs. It is also appropriate for
reading-disabled young adults.

Verheyden-Hilliard, Mary Ellen. Scientist from Puerto Rico,
María Cordero Hardy. (American Women in Science Biography) Bethesda, MD: The Equity Institute, Inc., 1985.
31 p. ISBN: 0-932469-02-7. $3.95. Gr. 3-5.

The purpose of this series is to encourage young readers
to make choices that help them achieve their own goals.
Thus, through the life of María Cordero, who was born in
Puerto Rico, children learn that despite a language barrier
and overt prejudice, a Puerto Rican woman can become a
scientist. There is nothing particularly exciting about
this biography, yet it may inspire some young Hispanic
readers to consider the choices in their own lives.

Wagenheim, Kal. Clemente! Maplewood, NJ: Waterfront
Press, 1984. 274 p. ISBN: 0-943862-18-3. $8.95.
Gr. 8-12.

This is a reprint of the 1973 edition which traces the life
of one of the greatest athletes in the history of baseball,
Roberto Clemente. Beginning with Clemente's childhood
in Puerto Rico, through his amazing career with the Pittsburgh Pirates, to his death in a plane crash in December,
1972, this biography will move all readers, especially baseball lovers. The few tiny and blurred, black-and-white
photographs of Clemente's personal and professional life
will not excite most readers.

SPAIN

*Albornoz, Miguel. Hernando de Soto: Knight of the Americas. Translated by Bruce Boeglin. New York: Franklin Watts, 1986. 389 p. ISBN: 0-531-15006-2. $18.95. Gr. 10-adult.

This is a romanticized biography of the Spanish conquistador and explorer, Hernando de Soto, by a well-known Ecuadorian writer and historian. Lovers of history and adventure will delight in De Soto's dangerous forays in Panama, Nicaragua and Peru as well as his difficult expedition to Florida and the discovery of the Mississippi River. In contrast to many Spanish conquistadores, De Soto exemplifies the best qualities of Spanish knights: courage, loyalty and fairness. Numerous footnotes and a most complete index and bibliography further add to the value of this exciting biography about a sympathetic and courageous man of his times.

Allen, John J. The Reconstruction of a Spanish Golden Age Playhouse: El Corral del Príncipe (1583-1744). Gainesville: University of Florida, 1983. 129 p. ISBN: 0-8130-0755-0. $25.00. Gr. 10-adult.

Serious students of theater of the Spanish Golden Age will be interested in this scholarly history and development of "El Corral del Príncipe." Based on facts, inference and conjecture, the author provides an erudite reconstruction of one of two permanent public theaters in Madrid for a century and a half. Black-and-white drawings, charts and attractive photographs add to the understanding of this important playhouse of Spanish theater.

Beaulac, Willard L. Franco: Silent Ally in World War II.
Carbondale: Southern Illinois University Press, 1986.
233 p. ISBN: 0-8093-1254-9. Gr. 9-adult.

Beaulac, a member of the U.S. diplomatic mission to
Spain during World War II, has written an engrossing
narrative which describes Hitler's efforts to entice or
coerce Spain into fighting for the Axis, while the Allies
sought to keep Franco's Spain neutral. This is a fast-
moving, pro-Spanish account of Spain's policy which was
aimed at frustrating German designs and keeping Spain
out of the war. Beaulac credits Spain for its ability to
carry out a policy that was unpopular and difficult and
which may have altered the course of World War II. It
also includes complimentary chapters on Franco; Spain's
foreign ministers: Beigbeder, Serrano and Jordana; the
British ambassador to Spain, Hoare; and the American
ambassadors, Weddell and Hayes.

*Bristow, Richard. We Live in Spain. New York: The
Bookwright Press, distributed by Franklin Watts and
Company, 1984. 64 p. (A Living Here Book) ISBN:
0-531-04780-6. $10.00. Gr. 6-12.

Through twenty-eight first-person interviews of Spanish
people of all ages, interests, occupations and backgrounds,
young readers are exposed to life in modern Spain. In
a most personal manner, people relate their problems with
the government in Madrid, their lives as flamenco dancers,
bullfighters, teachers, members of the civil guard and many
others. The outstanding photographs in color and the
honest and well-selected interviews make this an excellent
portrait of life in Spain in the 1980s.

*Brown, Jonathan. Velázquez: Painter and Courtier. New
Haven: Yale University Press, 1986. 322 p. ISBN:
0-300-03466-0. $45.00. Gr. 9-adult.

Professor Jonathan Brown from the Institute of Fine Arts,
New York University, has put together an exquisite book
that considers the great Spanish painter, Velázquez, both
from an artistic and a biographical point of view. The
excellent quality of the more than three hundred color and

black-and-white plates provides the novice with a fascinating
view of the art of this brilliant painter. In addition,
Brown's readable narrative is an engrossing analysis of
Velázquez's art and of seventeenth century painting and
theory. Art lovers and others will not be disappointed
in this stirring account on the life and art of one of the
greatest Spanish painters and of the society which produced him.

*Calderón de la Barca, Pedro. Guárdate de la agua mansa
(Beware of Still Waters). Translated by David M. Gitlitz.
San Antonio, TX: Trinity University Press, 1984. 201 p.
ISBN: 0-939980-04-5. $25.00. Gr. 9-adult.

This lighthearted comedy of intrigue and love is a marvelous introduction to the plays of the Spanish Golden Age
for adolescents. It includes the Spanish version, a most
enjoyable English translation on the opposite page, and
a clear, explicit introduction to the play and the characters. Readers and/or listeners will enjoy a father's unsuccessful attempts to marry off his daughters to whom
he believes are the best suitors. The supposedly saintly
oldest daughter, Clara, thinks otherwise and ultimately
achieves what she wants.

Calderón de la Barca, Pedro. Three Comedies. Translated
by Kenneth Muir and Ann L. Mackenzie. Lexington:
University Press of Kentucky, 1985. 206 p. ISBN:
0-8131-1546-9. $25.00. Gr. 9-adult.

These three early comedies by Calerdón de la Barca--
A House with Two Doors Is Difficult to Guard (Casa con
dos puertas mala es de guardar), Mornings of April and
May (Mañanas de abril y mayo), and No Trifling with
Love (No Hay burlas con el amor)--should appeal to young
adults much more than his more serious, though better
known, works. They are cloak-and-sword amusing
comedies with numerous clandestine amorous intrigues and
duels. The translation, which contains a mixture of prose
and verse, is light and cheerful. More serious students
will be interested in the informative and scholarly introduction and notes to the plays.

*Cervantes, Miguel de. The Adventures of Don Quixote de la Mancha. Translated by Tobias Smollett. New York: Farrar, Straus, Giroux, 1986. 846 p. ISBN: 0-374-14232-7. $25.00. Gr. 9-adult.

In the foreword, Carlos Fuentes states that this translation "is the homage of a novelist to a novelist.... Its immediacy and force, its playfulness and its freshness, will show the modern English language reader why Don Quixote is the first modern novel, perhaps the most eternal novel ever written..." (p. xiii). In addition to the captivating translation, this volume includes an informative account of the life of Cervantes which is not readily available to English readers. English readers who are ready to read this masterpiece of the Spanish language, will definitely enjoy and admire this translation.

Cervantes, Miguel de. Don Quixote. (Classics for Kids Series) Adapted by Joanne Fink. Illustrated by Hieronimus Fromm. Morristown, NJ: Silver Burdett Company, 1985. 31 p. ISBN: 0-382-06957-9. $4.47. Gr. 3-5.

The purpose of this series is to introduce young readers to the classics of literature through simple, easy-to-read texts and colorful illustrations. But, judging from this title, this series is an unfortunate mishap: It only offers the essence of the plot without the excitement of the original novel. Moreover, the garish illustrations are silly caricatures of Cervantes's well-known characters. This series is also available in Spanish.

Cohen, Matt. The Spanish Doctor. New York: Beaufort Books, 1984. 344 p. ISBN: 0-8253-0227-7. $16.95. Gr. 9-adult.

The persecution and suffering of European Jews in the fourteenth and fifteenth centuries are the background to this exciting novel which includes much passion, explicit sex and gory violence. Avram Halevi, son of a Jewish mother, was forced to convert to Catholicism at the age of seven. His successes as a doctor and scientist and his personal tribulations are excellently depicted as well as the life of European Jews and the power of the Catholic Church in Spain. What many readers might object to are

the sometimes complicated escapes, captures and violence.
This is, however, an engrossing novel with a sumptuous
historical background of Jewish life before the Renaissance.

The Defiant Muse: Hispanic Feminist Poems from the Middle
    Ages to the Present--A Bilingual Anthology. Edited by
    Angel Flores and Kate Flores. New York: The Feminist
    Press, 1986. 149 p. ISBN: 0-935312-54-4. $11.95.
    Gr. 9-adult.

According to the editors, feminist poetry "is a criticism
of women's lives, and of the injustices women have suffered, in various times and places, as a consequence of
their sex." This anthology contains old songs and ballads
from the thirteenth century as well as thirty-three female
poets from Spain and Latin America including such well-
known poets as Sor Juana Inés de la Cruz, Gabriela Mis-
tral, Alfonsina Storni, Rosario Castellanos, Gloria Fuertes
and others that have never been mentioned in histories
of Hispanic literature. The well-done English translations
and the power of the poems selected will definitely impress
upon the reader "the drama of women's struggle for their
rights in the Hispanic world."

*Descharnes, Robert. Salvador Dalí: The work, the man.
    Translated from the French by Eleanor R. Morse. New
    York: Harry N. Abrams, Inc., 1984. 456 p. ISBN:
    0-8109-0825-5. $145.00. Gr. 9-adult.

This expensive and exquisitely illustrated book includes
over 650 outstanding large color plates as well as numerous black-and-white and color photos, drawings and
documentary articles of the well-known surrealist painter
and designer, Salvador Dali. Each chapter is introduced
by a page or two of text followed by a chronological view
of Dali's work. Admirers of Dali will certainly appreciate
this prodigious book; only the price should discourage
many from acquiring it.

Dominigo, Plácido. My First Forty Years. New York:
    Alfred A. Knopf, 1983. 256 p. ISBN: 0-394-52329-6.
    $7.95. Gr. 9-adult.

The great Spanish opera singer Plácido Domingo relates
in a refreshing and enthusiastic manner his life as performer in opera and concerts all over the world as well
as his incredible schedule of recording sessions, filmings,
television appearances and interviews. Of special interest
to young adults are his early years in Spain, where he
was born; his youth in Mexico City where he tells about
his first unsuccessful marriage at age 16, fatherhood at
17, his successful second marriage to singer Marta Ornelas;
and his initial appearances as a performer in Mexico City,
Tel Aviv and New York City. After that, the world of
opera--directors, conductors, singers, opera houses,
orchestras--dominate the narrative, making this biography
of greater interest to confirmed opera lovers.

Evrard, Gaëtan. How I Cured Don Quixote by Doctor Sancho
Panza. Illustrated by the author. English Adaptation by
Paula Franklin. Morristown, NJ: Silver Burdett Company,
1986. [34 p.] ISBN: 0-382-09305-4. $10.45. Gr. 3-5.

The excitement of Cervantes's Don Quixote is certainly
lost in this bland attempt to offer a modern explanation to
Don Quixote's peculiar behavior. The powerful pastel illustrations have maintained the flavor of the beloved tale,
but the absurd plot will disappoint most readers. In this
version, Don Quixote mistakes monks for bandits, sheep for
enemy soldiers and windmills for wicked giants because he
is nearsighted. Neither Sancho Panza as doctor nor a
cured Don Quixote with glasses will convince young readers.

García Lorca, Federico. Selected Letters. New York: New
Direction, distributed by Norton & Co., 1983. 172 p.
ISBN: 0-8112-0872-9. $15.95. Gr. 10-adult.

Over one hundred of García Lorca's letters from age
twenty to a month before his execution by Granadan Fal-
angists at the age of thirty-nine have been translated and
edited by David Gershator. In addition, it includes an
introduction which provides a brief summary of García
Lorca's life and work. The letters reveal aspects of the
poet's literary life and his relationship with famous artists
of his time as Manuel de Falla, Jorge Guillén and several
of his childhood friends.

Gilmour, David. <u>The Transformation of Spain: from Franco to the Constitutional Monarchy.</u> London: Quartet Books Limited, 1985, dist. by Merrimack Publishers' Circle. 322 p. ISBN: 0-7043-2461-X. $19.95. Gr. 10-adult.

In a dry and monotonous manner, the author analyzes the years from 1975 until 1979 in which Spain transformed itself "radically but peacefully, with scarcely any interruption in the lives of its inhabitants. Political liberty had been legalized, human freedoms and the rights of regional minorities had been recognized. Above all, sovereignty had been restored to the people, whom the government had consulted regularly about the changes" (p. 269). For those English readers eager to get facts about political developments in Spain just after Franco's death, this book may provide basic information.

*Graham, Robert. <u>Spain: A Nation Comes of Age.</u> New York: St. Martin's Press, 1984. 327 p. ISBN: 0-312-74958-9. $14.95. Gr. 9-adult.

This is a most insightful commentary and analysis on the evolution of modern Spanish society written by Graham, who was the <u>Financial Times</u> of London correspondent in Madrid from 1977 to 1982. In an objective and serious manner, the author describes the changes in Spain from 1939 when Spain was a rural society devastated by a brutal civil war, to the social and economic changes of the 1950s up to the social, political and economic forces of the 1980s. Graham must be especially commended for his objective treatment of Franco's contributions to modern Spain as well as Franco's failures: "Franco cannot escape the damning criticism that he showed absolutely no magnanimity in victory and consciously rules over a divided country. The stability he provided was at a high cost in political, social and economic terms. The political life of Spain was suffocated. A system that rewards loyalty above initiative and that prizes conformity above individuality fosters a numbing mediocrity. Mediocrity was the stamp of the Franco era" (p. 23).

*Hancock, Sibyl. <u>Esteban and the Ghost.</u> Illustrated by Dirk Zimmer. New York: Dial Books for Young Readers, 1983. [32 p.] ISBN: 0-8037-2443-8. $10.95. Gr. 3-5.

Esteban, a merry tinker, hears a fabulous tale about a
haunted castle near Toledo in Spain. He decides to go to
the castle and try for the thousand gold reales which are
offered by the owner of the castle if he can drive the
ghost away. Esteban's good humor and delightful common
sense will charm readers; the black line drawings with
full-color illustrations add a sense of excitement to this
ghost tale without undue horror or violence.

Hemingway, Ernest. The Dangerous Summer. New York:
Charles Scribner's Sons, 1985. 228 p. ISBN: 0-684-
18355-2. $17.95. Gr. 8-adult.

The drama and excitement of bullfighting are recreated
by Ernest Hemingway as he chronicles the rivalry between
two great bullfighters, Antonio Ordóñez and Luis Miguel
Dominguín, in Spain in 1959. Bullfight aficionados and
Hemingway admirers will be enthralled by the descriptions
of the sights and people of Spain as they enjoy the thril-
ling art of bullfighting. A lengthy introduction by James
A. Michener provides interesting information about Hemingway, the author, and about bullfighting for the inexper-
ienced. Some readers might be repulsed by the seemingly
gory aspects of bullfighting, but the human dramas re-
vealed are a testimony to Hemingway's knowledge and interest in bullfighting.

*Herrera, Emilio. Flying: The Memoirs of a Spanish Aeronaut.
Translated by Elizabeth Ladd. Albuquerque: University
of New Mexico Press, 1984. 231 p. ISBN: 0-8263-0753-1.
$9.95. Gr. 8-12.

Emilio Herrera (1879-1967) displays his wit and sense of
humor in these amusing memoirs in which he tells about
his involvement in the early days of aviation in Spain.
He recounts experiments with hydrogen balloons, dirigibles
and the space suit as well as the scientific debates of his
time. In addition, he provides a sad view in the lives of
many frustrated Spanish scientists, who ended their professional lives in exile due to the tragedies of the Spanish
Civil War. This is a humorous and refreshingly honest
autobiography of a daring engineer and scientist.

*Horward, Donald D. Napoleon and Iberia: The Twin Sieges of Ciudad Rodrigo and Almeida, 1810. Gainesville, FL: University Presses of Florida, 1984. 419 p. ISBN: 0-8130-0793-3. $29.50. Gr. 10-adult.

The collapse of the Napoleonic Empire began with Napoleon's ill-conceived intervention in Iberia in 1810. Based on original correspondence, the author reconstructs the events which led up to the defenses of Ciudad Rodrigo and Almeida, analyzes the strategy and tactics of the combatants and offers candid insights into the personal aspirations and rivalries of some of the commanders of both armies, including Masséna, Wellington, Junot and others. Numerous maps and photographs add to the explanations of this detailed narrative on siege warfare of the period. This is exciting and informative reading for serious readers of European history in the nineteenth century.

Hunter, Stephen. The Spanish Gambit. New York: Crown Publishers, Inc. 1985. 387 p. ISBN: 0-517-55731-2. $15.95. Gr. 9-adult.

Intrigue, espionage, adventure, sex, and love are exquisitely intermingled in this novel set in Britain and Spain during the brutal years of the Spanish Civil War. As a powerful novel of suspense with well-developed male and female characters, this novel is sure to appeal to young adults. As a novel about the Spanish Civil War, however, it will disappoint many readers: It barely discusses the issues or circumstances of the times, the Spanish language is constantly misspelled and/or misused, and Spanish people are ignored.

*Jiménez, Juan Ramón. Platero and I. Translated by Eloïse Roach. Austin: University of Texas Press, 1983. 218 p. ISBN: 0-292-76479-0. $6.95. Gr. 8-adult.

This is an excellent translation of the classic work by the Spanish Nobel Prize-winning author, Juan Ramón Jiménez. It is a lyric portrait of life in a remote Andalusian village in which the author exchanges comments about nature with Platero, a donkey, a symbol of creation.

Knowlton, Mary Lee, and Mark J. Sachner, eds. Spain.
 (Children of the World) Photographs by Masami Yokoyama.
 Milwaukee: Gareth Stevens Publishing, 1987, 64 p. ISBN:
 1-5532-163-1. $12.45. Gr. 3-6.

Through Felisa, a twelve-year-old girl from Almonte, a
village in southern Spain, children are introduced to life
in rural Spain. Felisa is shown at home with her family,
at school, at play and participating in a Spanish religious
festival. A reference section at the end of the book describes the history, government, language, religion, art,
culture and other basic facts about Spain. Numerous
color photographs of Felisa in her small Spanish village
complement the text.

Kozinn, Alan, and others. The Guitar: The History, the
 Music, the Players. New York: William Morrow and
 Company, 1984. 208 p. ISBN: 0-688-01972-2. $24.00.
 Gr. 9-adult.

The first chapter of this book--"the Classical Guitar"--
will be of interest to lovers of the Spanish guitar and its
outstanding musicians. Numerous photographs and a
lively text tell the history of the classical guitar and how
renowned guitarists such as Fernando Sor ("the Beethoven
of the guitar"), Andrés Segovia, Narciso Yepes, Alexandre
Lagoya and John Williams have developed their techniques
and instruments. It also includes chapters on blues, jazz,
country, and rock. Each chapter concludes with a dis-
cography on inprint albums as well as a list of mail order
sources.

Lepscky, Ibi. Pablo Picasso. Translated from Italian by
 Howard Rodger MacLean. Illustrated by Paolo Cardoni.
 Woodbury, NY: Barron's Educational Services, 1984.
 24 p. ISBN: 0-8120-5511-X. $6.95. Gr. 1-3.

Picasso is introduced to young readers through a series
of temper tantrums, moody episodes and unexciting color
illustrations. There is nothing in this biography that
conveys Picasso's contributions to modern art. It will
bore and confuse all children.

*Love Poems from Spain and Spanish America. Selected and
  Translated by Perry Higman. San Francisco: City Lights
  Books, 1986. 243 p. ISBN: 0-87286-183-X. $7.95. Gr.
  8-adult.

Thirty-one poets and a few anonymous ballads from Spain
and Spanish America are represented in this bilingual
anthology of love poems. The selector/translator has done
an excellent job in re-creating the original poems for the
English reader. The poems explore many kinds of love as
well as feelings of friendship, solidarity, and altruistic
love of mankind. Admirers of Hispanic poets will delight
in some of these selections; others will be charmed by the
varied expressions of love from the 16th century to our
times.

Moon, Bernice and Cliff. Spain Is My Country. (My Country) New York: Marshall Cavendish, 1986. 64 p. ISBN:
  0-86307-469-3. $10.00. Gr. 3-6.

Through twenty-eight first-person accounts, young readers
will learn about life in the city, coast and countryside of
Spain. Carefully selected photographs in color and a
simple text describe the life of a dancer, restaurant owner,
bullfighter, nurse, mining engineer, lottery salesman,
artist, fisherman, teacher and many others. This is a
pleasant way to expose young readers to life in Spain.

Myers, Walter Dean. Adventure in Granada. New York:
  Puffin Books, 1985. 87 p. ISBN: 0-14-032011-3. $3.95.
  Gr. 5-9.

Young readers eager for a fast-paced novel that includes
adventure, excitement and intrigue will enjoy this novel
about two fourteen-year-old boys, Ken and Pedro, and
seventeen-year-old Chris. Ken and Chris are brothers
and Pedro is their Gypsy friend who they met in Spain.
Even though there is not much depth here, the Spanish
setting, the good-natured boys and their struggles with
sophisticated art smugglers and the Spanish police will
maintain the interest of the most reluctant reader.

O'Dell, Scott. The Castle in the Sea. Boston: Houghton
Mifflin Company, 1983. 184 p. ISBN: 0-395-34831-5.
$12.95. Gr. 8-12.

Young and beautiful, Lucinda de Cabrillo y Benivides is
also the richest or one of the richest girls in the world
after the tragic death of her authoritarian Spanish father.
Her life in the great stone castle becomes a nightmare as
she seems to be followed by a series of unexplained "acci-
dents." The touch of the master storyteller is obviously
there, amid a romantic story with lots of suspension and
excitement. What is most annoying, however, are the
ludicrous caricatures that all of the Spanish characters
in this story represent: The absolute villain, Ricardo
Villaverde, a former servant, dresses in absurd Spanish
costumes. Lucinda's fiancé, Porfirio de Puertoblanco, whom
she had never met, is vain, pompous and arrogant. And
the Spanish women, Doña Octavia and Doña Catalina, are
stiff and insensitive. Even though young readers are
supposed to acquire a dose of Spanish history which is
interspersed in the story, they will be especially affected
by the "absurdity" of Spanish people and customs as
described by O'Dell.

*Palau I Fabre, Josep. Picasso. New York: Rizzoli Inter-
national Publications, Inc., 1985. [127 p.] ISBN: 0-8478-
0652-9. $14.95. Gr. 8-adult.

A brief and insightful introductory essay to Picasso's life
and work as well as 150 reproductions (mostly in color)
of Picasso's paintings including a few examples of his col-
lages and sculptures make this book a rewarding introduction to this great master of modern art. In addition, the
short and simple interpretive notes about each reproduction
contribute to the readers' appreciation of Picasso's talents
and growth as an artist. The reasonable cost of this art
book is a welcome bonus.

Preston, Paul. The Spanish Civil War, 1936-39. New York:
Grove Press, Inc., 1986. 184 p. ISBN: 0-394-62274-X.
$20.00. Gr. 9-adult.

Preston compares the leftist defeat in Spain, 1936-1939,

to "the national liberation struggles in Vietnam, Cuba,
Chile and Nicaragua" (p. 2), and states that the Spanish
war "arose out of the violent opposition of the privileged
and their foreign allies to the reformist attempts of liberal
Republican-Socialist governments to ameliorate the daily
living conditions of the most wretched members of society"
(p. 7). Readers interested in a vivid reconstruction of
the harsh realities of the war and the emergence of Franco's
dictatorship, will be moved by Preston's comprehensive
narrative and the realistic 160 black-and-white photographs
which provide a striking view of the horror, propaganda
and destruction that prevailed during the Spanish Civil
War.

*Russell, P. E. Cervantes. (Past Masters Series) New York:
   Oxford University Press, 1985. 117 p. ISBN: 019-
   287570-1. $14.95. Gr. 9-adult.

This book, intended for English-speaking readers, relates
Don Quixote and other literary endeavors to Cervantes's
own life. Clearly and logically, Professor Russell demonstrates the ambivalence inherent in Don Quixote and explains
why so many generations have found in Cervantes's masterpiece a mirror of their own preoccupations. In addition,
Professor Russell argues most convincingly how Cervantes
proved that great art could be comic art. Serious students
of Cervantes will find this a most insightful and informative
study.

Secrest, Meryle. Salvador Dalí. New York: E. P. Dutton
   & Co., Inc., 1986. 307 p. ISBN: 0-535-24459-X. $22.50.
   Gr. 10-adult.

Meryle Secrest attempts to explain, in this in-depth biography, how many of Dalí's outbursts and emotional crises
were either sheer braggadocio or clear fabrication. She
writes about truths in Dalí's life that he might have tried
to conceal. And, she tries to make a judicious assessment
of Dalí's genius. Thus, the reader is presented with a
most intimate biography of the controversial surrealist
painter with details of his troubled childhood, early friends,
his impact on the Paris Surrealists, his marriage to the
popular Gala, his middle age and his dotage. Perhaps some

readers might be perplexed by the author's extensive psychoanalyzing of Dalí's actions and behavior; nevertheless, this is an enlightening and forthright account of the artist and his times.

Snowman, Daniel. The World of Plácido Domingo. New York: McGraw-Hill Book Company, 1985. 298 p. ISBN: 0-07-059527-5. $15.95. Gr. 9-adult.

Most of this book describes the great opera singer Plácido Domingo at work. The author follows Domingo "at the height of his powers as he devotes hour after hour, day after day, to the painstaking process of working on a new role or production or polishing a familiar one, gradually building it up until it is ready to be unveiled before the public" (p. 3). There is no question that opera lovers and especially, fans of the operatic superstar will enjoy this admiring portrait of Plácido Domingo; others will prefer a more straightforward biography with less psychoanalyzing about Domingo's tremendous personality and artistic abilities.

*Von Canon, Claudia. The Inheritance. Boston: Houghton Mifflin Company, 1983. 212 p. ISBN: 0-395-33891-3. $10.95. Gr. 8-12.

Miguel de Roxas is nineteen years old and a medical student in Padua in 1580. Unexpectedly, he learns that his father has died in the prison of the Spanish Inquisition. He returns home to Saragossa to claim his inheritance where he meets political intrigue and the full force of the Spanish Holy Office. Convinced of the horrors of the Inquisition, he flees Spain to find refuge and, eventually, romance in Basel, Switzerland. The drama, abuses and terror prevalent in the Spanish Court during the sixteenth century are masterfully recreated in this powerful novel with remarkably appealing characters. In addition, it provides genuine insights to the early practice of medicine in Europe during those turbulent years.

Walters, D. Gareth. Francisco de Quevedo, Love Poet. Washington: The Catholic University of America Press, 1985. 185 p. ISBN: 0-7083-0899-6. $24.95. Gr. 10-adult.

This is an in-depth, extremely well-documented study whose purpose is to define the ethos behind the linguistic brilliance of Quevedo's love poetry. The author demonstrates Quevedo's thematic individuality by close attention to a number of hitherto neglected poems and by comparison with the works of Quevedo's immediate predecessors and contemporaries. Non-Spanish readers will benefit by the author's translations of Quevedo's verse into English prose. Only the most devoted admirers of Quevedo's poetry will have the background to benefit from this scholarly study and criticism of Quevedo's love poetry.

Anaya, Rudolfo A., and Antonio Márquez, eds. <u>Cuentos</u>
<u>Chicanos: A Short Story Anthology</u>. Rev. ed. Albu-
querque: University of New Mexico Press, 1984. 186 p.
ISBN: 0-8263-0772-8. $9.95. Gr. 10-adult.

These twenty-one short stories tell about the joys, con-
cerns, and sorrows of well-known Chicago authors such
as Rudolfo A. Anaya, Sergio Elizondo, Bruce-Novoa and
other emerging new writers. Three of the stories are in
Spanish, the rest are all in English. Some of the stories
deal with mature themes; others explore family relations
as well as Chicano cultural values and topics.

Ashabranner, Brent. <u>Dark Harvest: Migrant Farmworkers</u>
<u>in America</u>. Photographs by Paul Conklin. New York:
Dodd, Mead & Company, 1985. 109 p. ISBN: 0-396-
08624-1. $13.95. Gr. 9-12.

This is a monotonous, rambling indictment against American
agribusiness and the U.S. government. The author concludes that a "system is evil that forces children to spend
their lives in manual labor, that pays little attention to
health and safety standards, that holds human beings in
peonage, that welcomes illegal aliens because of the low
wages they will take, that brings foreign laborers into the
country to take jobs away from its citizens" (p. 107).
There is no question that the author has described with
much compassion the tragic world of migrant farmworkers
in America. He does not, however, demonstrate the same
compassion or understanding toward the illegal Mexican,
Central American, Haitian or Jamaican workers who also,
for their own tragic reasons, must live the lives of migrants

in this country. As a simple, passionate, journalistic
report, this may serve a purpose. It definitely is not,
however, an in-depth analysis of the many human, political and economic issues surrounding agriculture, migrant
workers and illegal immigration into the United States.

Brown, Tricia. Hello, Amigos! Photographs by Fran Ortiz.
New York: Henry Holt and Company, 1986. [44 p.]
ISBN: 0-8050-0090-9. $12.95. Gr. 1-3.

Frankie Valdez, a Mexican-American boy who lives in
San Francisco with his father, mother, brothers and sis-
ters, is eagerly anticipating his birthday party. Striking
black-and-white photos of Frankie at home, at school and
at the Boy's Club and a brief and sensitive text convey
Frankie's enthusiasm as he plays kickball at school, rushes
home for the party and breaks the piñata accompanied by
his family and friends. This story has many common
Mexican ingredients--frijoles, tortillas, mariachis, and
piñatas--as well as a few Spanish words interspersed in
the text. For these reasons, it may appeal to some readers
who wish to sample a "typical" Mexican birthday celebration.

*Cabeza de Vaca, Alvar Núñez. Adventures in the Unknown
Interior of America. Translated and annotated by Cyclone
Covey. Albuquerque: University of New Mexico Press,
1983. 160 p. ISBN: 0-8263-0656-X. $6.95. Gr. 9-adult.

The fascinating report of Cabeza de Vaca's wanderings
with three companions over six thousand miles and eight
years across Florida, Texas, New Mexico, Arizona and
northern Mexico in the 1500s is entertaining as well as
informative reading. For history lovers, it provides firsthand information on the pre-European Southwest, the
variety of its climate, its flora, its fauna and the customs
of its natives. Seekers of adventure will be enthralled by
Cabeza de Vaca's undertakings which include severe de-
privation, misery and suffering amidst the native American
people he met along his route. In the epilogue, William T.
Pilkington describes Cabeza de Vaca as deserving the dis-
tinction of being called the Southwest's first writer.

Chávez, Denise. The Last of the Menu Girls. Houston:
  Arte Público Press, 1986. 190 p. ISBN: 0-934770-46-8.
  $8.50. Gr. 10-adult.

Collection of seven stories that tell about Rocío Esquibel,
as a child, young woman, teacher and aspiring writer in
her native New Mexico. Mature readers might enjoy the
long interior monologues, imaginative world and flavor of
southern New Mexico intermixed with a strong dose of
Spanish.

Day, Carol Olsen, and Edmund Day. The New Immigrants.
  (An Impact Book). New York: Franklin Watts, 1985.
  119 p. ISBN: 0-531-04929-9. $10.90. Gr. 7-12.

The problems of legal and illegal migration into the U.S.
are examined in a careful and well-organized manner. The
authors describe the experiences of immigrants from Latin
America, Asia, Haiti and the Soviet Union and explain why
they chose or were forced to come to the U.S. Also, they
explain some of the ways that these immigrants affect the
U.S. and the many issues--political, social, economic, and
humanitarian--that must be addressed as the U.S. develops
a new immigration policy. Some experts in the field of
immigration disagree with the authors' contention that
immigrants have a negative effect on the U.S. economy,
and others may question the authors' strong support of
the Simpson-Mazzoli Bill. Notwithstanding the controversial
positions taken by the authors, this is a well-thought-out
analysis and description of a serious contemporary pro-
blem.

Diehl, Kemper, and Jan Jarboe. Cisneros: Portrait of a
  New American. San Antonio, TX: Corona Publishing Co.,
  1985. 160 p. ISBN: 0-931722-35-7. $16.95. Gr. 9-
  adult.

The authors, two Texas journalists, have written a most
sympathetic political biography of the San Antonio mayor
who was also considered as a Democratic vice-presidential
candidate in 1984. There is no question that the authors
believe that an important political future lies ahead for
Cisneros and that he excels in all personal attributes.

They describe his style: "Call it charisma. Call it force
of personality or pizazz. Call it whatever you want. But
whatever it is, Cisneros has it" (p. 13). In addition,
they describe Cisneros as a most attractive human being
and "a politician with high purpose, and idealist who
knows the ropes" (p. 142), and so forth.

Fife, Dale H. Rosa's Special Garden. Illustrated by Marie
DeJohn. Niles, IL: Albert Whitman & Company, 1985.
[28 p.] ISBN: 0-8075-7115-6. $9.25. Gr. K-2.

Even though Rosa is too little to have a garden of her
own, she gets one corner of the yard, near a brick wall,
which she makes into a place for animals and people to
visit. Neither the realistic three-tone illustrations of Rosa
and her family working in the garden nor the textbook-like
text are particularly exciting; nevertheless, this is an
adequate story about springtime and a loving, though
bland, Hispanic family.

*Jakes, John. Susanna of the Alamo: A True Story.
Illustrated by Paul Bacon. San Diego: Harcourt Brace
Jovanovich, 1986. [30 p.] ISBN: 0-15-200592-7. $13.95.
Gr. 3-6.

This is a stirring account of the fall of the Alamo in 1836
in which all of the white male defenders were killed by
orders of Mexico's traitorous dictator, General Santa Anna.
Young readers will be moved by Susanna Dickinson, a
young mother, who was freed by Santa Anna to deliver a
letter to Sam Houston advising no further resistance. The
succinct, slightly romanticized text, and the moving, soft
watercolor-and-line artwork give the reader a touching
account of the massacre that resulted in the deaths of many
heroes including Davy Crockett, Jim Bowie and William
Barrett Travis.

MacMillan, Diane, and Dorothy Freeman. My Best Friend
Martha Rodríguez: Meeting a Mexican-American Family.
Illustrated by Warren Fricke. New York: Julian Messner,
1986. 47 p. ISBN: 0-671-61973-X. $9.29. Gr. 3-5.

Through Kathy, an American girl, and Martha, a Mexican-
American girl, young readers are introduced to Mexican-
American customs and beliefs, such as a birthday party,
a funeral, "Las Posadas," and others. As a superficial
introduction to Mexican-American traditions, this book
may serve a purpose. But, unfortunately, it reinforces
many stereotypes of poor Mexican-American people--over-
crowded living conditions, constant partying--as well as
incorrect Spanish grammar: "Mucho gusto conocerle"
[sic] (pp. 32 & 35). The black-and-white illustrations
portray a variety of Mexican people involved in "typical"
Mexican activities.

Paine, Lauran. The New Mexico Heritage. New York:
Walker and Company, 1987. 202 p. ISBN: 0-8027-
0940-0. $15.95. Gr. 8-adult.

Life on a ranch in New Mexico in the late nineteenth century is vividly recreated in this Walker Western mystery.
Dr. George Brunner saves the life of the heroine, beautiful
Maria Antonia Gallegos Lord, who was shot at her father's
funeral. Suspenseful action, strong characters, and a
lively dialogue make this a most enjoyable Western with
an uplifting Hispanic flavor.

*Pascoe, Elaine. Racial Prejudice. (Issues in American
History) New York: Franklin Watts, Inc., 1985. 118 p.
ISBN: 0-531-10057-X. $10.90. Gr. 7-12.

This is a most convincing and understandable narrative
that explains why "racial prejudice is the most vicious
and most difficult form" of prejudice to do away with.
It explores some of the underpinnings of racial prejudice
in the United States and examines how prejudices developed
against different groups--blacks, Indians, Orientals and
Hispanics. Even though the prejudice against blacks is
examined in greater detail than the other groups, the
author provides enough background information "to understand how prejudice formed against these groups, what
factors worked to perpetuate it, and how each of the
groups has worked to overcome it" (p. 16).

Paulsen, Gary. Sentries. New York: Bradbury Press. 1986. 165 p. ISBN: 0-02-770100-X. $11.95. Gr. 7-10.

Brief vignettes in the lives of a native American girl, an illegal Mexican migrant worker, the daughter of a sheep rancher, a rock musician and three war veterans are included in this collection of stories that do not add up to a novel. David Garcia, a fourteen-year-old Mexican boy, is supposed to represent the suffering of the migrant workers in the U.S. Gradually, and with some misspelled Spanish words thrown in for "authenticity," he learns that he isn't as lucky as he initially thought he was. These are superficial vignettes with a great number of minority characters thrown in for effect.

Perrigo, Lynn I. Hispanos: Historic Leaders in New Mexico. Santa Fe: Sunstone Press, 1985. 94 p. ISBN: 0-86534-011-0. $9.95. Gr. 9-adult.

A sampling of the careers of twenty-seven eminent Hispanos is interwoven with the history of New Mexico in this unassuming paperback publication. A few nondescript black-and-white photographs add a much-needed authenticity to this brief historical report about the lives and actions of New Mexico's leading citizens.

Roberts, Maurice. César Chávez and La Causa. Chicago: Children's Press, 1986. 32 p. ISBN: 0-516-03484-7. $7.95. Gr. 3-5.

In a straightforward, direct style, this brief biography tells the life of César Chávez, the founder and leader of the United Farm Workers of America. Numerous black-and-white photographs of César Chávez and his family and his various activities in support of his struggle "for human rights and dignity of migrant and farm workers" emphasize Chávez's dedication to La Causa.

Roberts, Maurice. Henry Cisneros: Mexican-American Mayor. Chicago: Children's Press, 1986. 32 p. ISBN: 0-516-03485-5. $7.95. Gr. 3-5.

Henry Cisneros, the first American of Mexican descent
ever elected mayor of an important city--San Antonio,
Texas--is the product of his middle-class background which
values education and hard work. Numerous black-and-
white photographs, a straightforward text that highlights
Cisneros' achievements in politics and a large print result in an easy-to-read biography about a young Mexican-
American politician.

Sheridan, Thomas E. Los Tucsonenses: The Mexican Community in Tucson, 1854-1941. Tucson: The University of
Arizona Press, 1986. 327 p. ISBN: 0-8165-0876-3.
$22.50. Gr. 10-adult.

The contributions of the Mexican community in Tucson are
amply demonstrated in this scholarly historical narrative,
written by an assistant ethnohistorian at the Arizona
State Museum. Based on statistical archives and pioneer
reminiscences, the author demonstrates that "Tucson supported a strong Mexican middle class of businessmen, pro-
fessionals, artists, and intellectuals. Furthermore, its
proximity to Sonora allowed many Mexican families to
maintain close ties with their mother country, buffering
them against the psychological stresses of immigration.
With its elite families, its elegant theaters, its vigorous
mutualista movement and its active Spanish-language press,
Tucson's Mexican community served as a haven for Hispanic society and culture in the Southwest" (p. 240).
Maps, charts and black-and-white photographs accompany
this well-researched document on the Mexican community
of Tucson.

Soto, Gary. Small Faces. Arte Público, University of
Houston, 1986. 126 p. ISBN: 0934770-49-2. $8.00.
Gr. 9-12.

Thirty-one brief "prose reminiscences" are included in
this collection in which the author reflects on Mexicans,
Okies, poverty, family and friends. These are personal
and candid views on life that emphasize the value and
importance of human relationships.

*Taha, Karen T. A Gift for Tía Rosa. Illustrated by Dee
   de Rosa. Minneapolis: Dillon Press, Inc., 1986. 38 p.
   ISBN: 0-87518-306-9. $10.95 Gr. 3-5.

Carmela, a loving Hispanic girl, is eagerly awaiting the
return of her elderly aunt and neighbor, Tía Rosa, who
is very sick. Even though Tía Rosa must stay in bed,
she still wants to knit and talk to Carmela. When Tía
Rosa dies, Carmela is distraught, but finally manages to
accept Tía Rosa's death and complete Tía Rosa's half-
finished blanket for her new granddaughter. Children
will be touched by this warm story that deals directly
with death and grief. Sensitive water-color illustrations
of a Hispanic family provide an affectionate background
to the story.

*Weisman, Alan. La Frontera: The United States Border
   with Mexico. Photographs by Jay Dusard. San Diego:
   Harcourt Brace Jovanovich, 1986. 200 p. ISBN: 0-15-
   147315-3. $29.95. Gr. 9-adult. (See review under
   "Mexico")

VENEZUELA

Kurusa. The Streets Are Free. Illustrated by Monika
Doppert. Translated by Karen Englander. Scarborough,
Ontario: Annick Press, distr. by Firefly books, 1985.
[46 p.] ISBN: 0-920303-09-9. $8.95. Gr. 3-6.

Originally published in Spanish, this realistic story,
with vivid illustrations, depicts life in the slums of
Caracas, Venezuela. It tells how a group of children,
who did not have a place to play, organized their whole
neighborhood and constructed their own park on an
empty lot. Latin American young readers, who know the
problems of police abuse and bureaucratic indifference,
will empathize with the children in this story.

AUTHOR INDEX

TITLE INDEX

.